AF591040

The Ark
The Flood
and
The Rainbow

Isaac Benjamin-Nyarko

Jesus Joy Publishing

First Published and printed in Great Britain in 2011 by
Jesus Joy Publishing, a division of Eklegein Ltd

ISBN 978-1-90797-108-2

Jesus Joy Publishing
A division of Eklegein Ltd
www.jesusjoypublishing.co.uk
20040913

Dedication

I dedicate this book to My Saviour, Lord and ever-enabling Shepherd, Jesus Christ. I am nothing without God, my Creator and it is by His awesome grace that I am alive today to testify that my beloved God is magnificent indeed. The Lord has done many wonderful things in my life; He is greatly to be praised.

Acknowledgement

First and foremost, I give all glory to my Lord Jesus Christ for making it possible for me to get this far. All my appreciation goes out to my King of glory for His awesome grace, His mercies and His uncommon favour upon my life. All thanks and praises to God for His faithfulness and His marvellous kindness. I bless the name of the Lord and may He be exalted forever and ever.

To my father, Elder J.M. Adade Nyarko, God bless you for your priceless fatherhood. Thank you for your friendship, wisdom and patience. God bless you for all your humility and the sacrifices you made for the sake of our family. Thank you for everything you taught me. The world is certainly a better place because of you. God bless you all the days of your life.

To my mother, Mrs. Victoria Lartey, God bless you for everything you have done for me. Thank you for all your support, love and protection. There were many near-death situations, but you were always there to pull me out by the grace of God. The world would not be the same without you. May God bless you all the days of your life.

To Mr Michael and Dr Mrs Carla Cornelius, of Jesus Joy Publishing. God bless you for your support and for helping me to make this dream come to pass to the glory of the Lord. May God bless you both all the days of your lives and may your ministry be blessed.

To everyone who sacrificed and stood in the gap to pray for me, God bless all of you and may all your prayers be answered. I also pray that God, who never fails, will cause miracles to rain down over your lives. God bless you all.

Contents

11 Preface

13 Chapter One
The Divine Plan

41 Chapter Two
The Ark

95 Chapter Three
The Flood

109 Chapter 4
The Rainbow

149 Chapter Five
Declaring The Awesomeness Of God

Preface

Without God we can do nothing: there is nothing that exists in the entire universe which can be compared to our eternal God and Father who never fails. God is more than anyone can ever imagine because He is the all-sufficient, incandescent God who is 'the ancient of days'. I am so convinced that there are no words which are good enough to totally explain the awesomeness of God. The existence of God cannot be explained, His power cannot be measured, His ways cannot be fully understood and His love is unmatchable.

Chapter One

The Divine Plan

God had a wonderful plan to create and build a world for creatures to inhabit to His glory. God was not in need of anything because He was God all by Himself and He will always be God whether He creates or not. God was already awesome, magnificent and miraculous—all by Himself even before He made anything. Nevertheless, He created us to love us with His perfect love.

The Beginning of All Things

> *"In the beginning God created the heavens and the earth. The earth was without form, and void; and darkness was on the face of the deep. And the Spirit of God was hovering over the face of the waters. Then God said "Let there be light"; and there was light. And God saw the light, that it was good; and God divided the light from the darkness. God called the light Day, and the darkness He called Night. So the evening and the morning were the first day."*
>
> *[Genesis 1:1-5]*

God gladly continued to build according to His

creative genius and He witnessed that everything He made was without fault. God saw His perfection in all that He designed with the Word of His mouth and He was well-pleased.

> *"Then God said 'Let there be a firmament in the midst of the waters, and let it divide the waters from the waters.' Thus God made the firmament, and divided the waters which were under the firmament from the waters which were above the firmament; and it was so. And God called the firmament Heaven. So the evening and the morning were the second day. Then God said, "Let the waters under the heavens be gathered together into one place, and let the dry land appear"; and it was so."*
>
> [Genesis 1:6-9]

God added more and more wonders to the number of phenomenal things He formed. Everything God created reflected His mystery and His beauty, and He continued to increase His creativity.

> *And God called the dry land Earth, and the gathering together of the waters He called Seas. And God saw that it was good. Then God said, "Let the earth bring forth grass, the herb that yields seed, and the fruit tree that yields fruit according to its*

kind, whose seed is in itself, on the earth"; and it was so. And the earth brought forth grass, the herb that yields seed according to its kind, and the tree that yields fruit, whose seed is in itself according to its kind. And God saw that it was good.

[Genesis 1:10-12]

At this point, God created herbs and vegetation as the source of food for both humans and animals as He knew that we were going to need food to survive. In addition, God thought of us when He caused the Earth to bring forth trees to bare fruits because He knew that we would feed on them to survive. The herbs were also created for medicinal purposes as God knew that there would be sicknesses as He foresaw that sin was going to enter the world. This shows the love of God towards us whom He created in His image. God already put things in place for all of us to help us.

So the evening and the morning were the third day. Then God said, "Let there be lights in the firmament of the heavens to divide the day from the night; and let them be for signs and seasons, and for days and years; and let them be for lights in the firmament of the heavens to give light on the earth"; and it was so.

Then God made two great lights: the greater light to rule the day, and the lesser light to rule the night. He made the stars also. God set them in the firmament of the heavens to give light on the earth, and to rule over the day and over the night, and to divide the light from the darkness. And God saw that it was good.

[Genesis 1:13-18]

This was when God created the sun to shine upon the Earth in the daytime and He created the moon to glow at night to give us light. Considering that the moon does not fully shine like the sun or produce as much energy, it gives us enough light which helps us to see at night. Apart from the sun and the moon, God created many more stars to shine upon the Earth to create light at night. Although, many of the stars are very distant in our galaxy, they produce enough light upon the Earth to beautify the night - almost like a fireworks display in the darkness of the sky.

Divine Arrangement

This was when God began to separate the high from the low and the low from the high. The Lord put everything according to the order of the design He had in His mind. God began to arrange things and decided where each creation would be and what their functions would be. God's perfect discipline and care is revealed in all of this because absolutely nothing was overlooked or misplaced. We can clearly see that the things which God created were specifically positioned in certain places for good reasons and we can also see that everything was interconnected - nothing could work by itself or for itself. For example, the sky was created to do many things, but we can also see that it exposes the sun for us. In addition, we know that the rays of the sun help to produce energy for the trees on the ground, which in turn, produce oxygen for human beings to breathe. Light was created to conquer darkness; however, without darkness there would be no need for light. We can also see that without the earth, trees and herbs could not grow. In the same manner, God created us to serve one another and to assist one another to accomplish God's purpose for our lives. In the Body of Christ, we are one; it is important to acknowledge that we need one another regardless of who we are, where we are or where we are from.

> *So the evening and the morning were the fourth day. Then God said, "Let the waters abound with*

> *an abundance of living creatures, and let birds fly above the earth across the face of the firmament of the heavens." So God created great sea creatures and every living thing that moves, with which the waters abounded, according to their kind, and every winged bird according to its kind. And God saw that it was good.*
>
> [Genesis 1:19-21]

This was when God created all the fish and the mammals that dwell in the sea and the birds that fly in the sky. The creatures in the sea were specially designed and shaped in such a way that they could survive perfectly in the oceans. But, they cannot survive on dry land. In addition, the creatures of the sky have the advantage of dwelling on dry land, build nests in trees and fly in the sky.

> *And God blessed them, saying, "Be fruitful and multiply, and fill the waters in the seas, and let birds multiply on the earth." So the evening and the morning were the fifth day. Then God said, "Let the earth bring forth the living creature according to its kind: cattle and creeping thing and beast of the earth, each according to its kind"; and it was so. And God made the beast of the earth according to*

its kind, cattle according to its kind, and everything that creeps on the earth according to its kind. And God saw that it was good.

[Genesis 1:22-25]

Now, we can see that God caused the Earth to produce creatures known as beasts to inhabit the earth. These creatures were different from the creatures in the sea and the ones in the air because they were designed to have legs, feet and backbone that they would walk on the earth. Apart from the beasts with legs and backbone, there were others without back bones such as reptiles that crawled and crept on the surface of the earth.

Everything God created has remained the same in the sense that the sky is still the sky and it has not changed into something else. The oceans are still oceans and they have not dried up into a desert. The earth is still the earth and it has not changed, the sun, the moon and the air in the atmosphere have not changed despite the curses that continue to occur as a result of the sin that has dominated life since the days of Adam and Eve. Light has remained light and darkness has remained darkness; eyes have not turned into ears and mouths have not turned into noses. Everything is still the same as God designed it to be and they all continue to function to God's glory. However, the only thing that continues to cause problems for God's creation is the power of sin. In addition, it was sin that brought imperfection into the life of every creature; therefore, our behaviour is contrary to what God intended in the beginning. Moreover, the Earth does not choose what it should grow and what not to grow, the sun does not stop shining and the moon does not stop glowing at night. This tells us that the power of God still controls the world - even if it appears as if it is not so.

In The Image Of God

> *Then God said, "Let Us make man in Our image, according to Our likeness; let them have dominion over the fish of the sea, over the birds of the air, and over the cattle, over all the earth and over every creeping thing that creeps on the earth." So God created man in His own image; in the image of God He created him; male and female He created them. Then God blessed them, and God said to them, "Be fruitful and multiply; fill the earth and subdue it; have dominion over the fish of the sea, over the birds of the air, and over every living thing that moves on*

the earth."

[Genesis 1:26-28]

This was the beginning of Adam and Eve who were designed according to the perfect image of God. The Lord was well pleased to create man in His image to dwell on Earth to represent Him. All God's creation was created with wonder, but man was "fearfully and wonderfully made". Everything that God produced with His mouth and His hands were unquestionably awesome because our God is a phenomenal Creator. There is no one like Him. It is extremely important to acknowledge God extensively; His ingenuity is unmatchable indeed. The Bible passage above tells us that God looked at everything which He created and declared that it was good. Everything that came out of God was good and absolutely useful. Nothing that God made was ever destructive because God is a purposeful God. God was very pleased with Himself because He admired His creation. In addition, God was more overjoyed to create man because He made them in His own image. God saw Himself in Adam and Eve because He made them according His character and attributes. However, the man and the woman whom God created so beautifully in His likeness, sinned against God when they failed to obey the only instruction they were given. The Bible records that

"When the woman saw that the fruit of the tree was good for food and pleasing to the eye, and also desirable for gaining wisdom, she took some and ate it. She also gave some to her husband, who was with her, and he ate it."

[Genesis 3:6]

This was what changed everything and launched mankind into something so unspeakable that if God refused to show mercy upon us, the world would have been hell on earth. Nevertheless, God did not destroy Adam and Eve, but He punished them. *[Genesis 3:1-24]* Notwithstanding, there came a time that God decided to implement a zero tolerance policy against the world when human beings became too evil.

"For you shall worship no other god, for the LORD, whose name is Jealous, is a jealous God."

[Exodus 34:14]

God does not share His glory with anyone because there is none like Him. God is the only true God who is worthy of all our worship and praise. God does not have to tolerate any activity which only brings disappointment and destroys what is profitable.

> *"Do not withhold correction from a child, for if you beat him with a rod, he will not die. You shall beat him with a rod, and deliver his soul from hell."*
>
> *[Proverbs 23: 13-14]*

A father becomes disheartened when his children do not conduct themselves appropriately. In the same manner, teachers can be ashamed when their students fail to perform well, especially when they invest an ample amount of time and effort to educate their pupils. God made the decision to destroy and rebuild, as His wrath had been awoken. God had already spared Adam and Eve, but this time He refused to spare because there was an overflow of evil.

> *For the creation was subjected to frustration, not by its own choice, but by the will of the one who subjected it, in hope that the creation itself will be liberated from its bondage to decay and brought into the freedom and glory of the children of God. We know that the whole creation has been groaning as in the pains of childbirth right up to the present time. Not only so, but we ourselves, who have the firstfruits of the Spirit, groan inwardly as we wait*

eagerly for our adoption to sonship, the redemption of our bodies.

[Romans 8:20-23]

Though, God's creation was good, it has been suffering because of the deficiency that continues to occur since the days of Adam and Eve. There are infirmities, horrific crimes that take place all over the world such as; larceny, crimes of arson, violent brawls etc. In the beginning, there was no such thing as emotional, physical and mental pain because God made all things good.

To Adam he said, "Because you listened to your wife and ate fruit from the tree about which I commanded you, 'You must not eat from it,' "Cursed is the ground because of you; through painful toil you will eat food from it all the days of your life. It will produce thorns and thistles for you, and you will eat the plants of the field. By the sweat of your brow you will eat your food until you return to the ground, since from it you were taken; for dust you are and to dust you will return."

[Genesis 3:17-19]

Ever since that time, mankind has been working extremely hard and sweating to eat, but in the beginning it was not so. All the hard work and struggles of mankind are a result of the curse which God pronounced upon the Earth. This is why there are crops that sometimes wither away without producing fruit. There are farms that experience severe droughts and reap minimum harvests as a result of pestilence. In addition, men, women and children die of diseases and severe conditions that are uncommon to man. There are also extreme storms that often devastate many parts of the Earth. Animals also die, either from diseases or as prey to other animals. Nevertheless, Jesus Christ is the perfect solution to all curses.

> *To the woman he said,"I will make your pains in childbearing very severe; with painful labour you will give birth to children. Your desire will be for your husband, and he will rule over you."*
>
> *[Genesis 3:16]*

The scripture alerts us to the reason why women experience severe pains and suffer in childbearing. Apart from giving birth, there are other painful and difficult things that women go through in their lifetime as a result of the curse which was spoken out of the mouth of God. However, the time will come when nothing on Earth will suffer any more. Christ will come back to make all things perfect again, and even the animal kingdom will be restored back to the way it was in the beginning before sin entered the world. The Bible tells us that

> *"The wolf also shall dwell with the lamb, the leopard shall lie down with the young goat, the calf and the young lion and the fatling together; and a little child shall lead them, the cow and the bear shall graze; Their young ones shall lie down together; and the lion shall eat straw like the ox. The nursing child shall play by the cobra's hole, and the weaned child shall put his hand in the viper's den. They shall not hurt nor destroy in all my holy mountain, for the earth shall be full of the knowledge of the Lord as the waters cover the sea."*
>
> *[Isaiah 11:6-9]*

Everything will come back to its original state according to how God made them in the beginning. Children will move freely without being afraid of the snake, the lion or the tiger. There will be divine peace in the world and the love of God will completely permeate the whole Earth as if nothing had happened at all.

The New Plan

> *"Then the LORD saw that the wickedness of man was great in the earth, and that every intent of the thoughts of his heart was only evil continually. And the LORD was **sorry** that He had made man on the earth, and He was grieved in His heart. So the LORD said 'I will destroy man whom I have created from the face of the earth, both man and beast, creeping thing and birds of the air, for I am sorry that I have made them."*
>
> *[Genesis 6:5-7, emphasis added]*

In the King James Version, the Bible tells us in Genesis 6 -

> *"And God saw that the wickedness of man was great in the earth, and that every imagination of the thoughts of his heart was only evil continually. And it repented the Lord that he had made man on the earth, and it grieved him at his heart. And the LORD said, I will destroy man whom I have created from the face of the earth; both man, and beast, and the creeping thing, and the fowls of the air; for it repenteth me that I have made them.*
>
> *[Genesis 6:5-7]*

Many Christians get very confused with this type

of ideology that God repented because repentance means 'change of mind and change of direction.' This does not mean that God is a changeable God; He does not change His mind as we do because He is perfect and holy. God does not repent like us, but in this case it means God was disheartened with the behaviour of mankind and was getting ready to put new things in place---that mankind would receive the Salvation of Christ. Let us be careful not to judge God or speak of Him as if He is like one of us.

> *Behold, I will do a new thing; now it shall spring forth; shall ye not know it? I will even make a way in the wilderness, and rivers in the desert.*
>
> *[Isaiah 43:19]*

This scripture confirms that God always plans to renew, restore and rebuild for our own benefit. This explains that God always has a plan to put things right. God knew that mankind was going to rebel against Him even before He created the world. However, it does not mean that the unrighteous ways of man did not grieve Him when He saw it happen. The New King James version says *"for I am sorry that I have made them."* But, the scripture is telling us that God was hurt to witness the evil that mankind did all over the Earth.

> *"God is not a man, that He should lie, nor a son of man, that He should repent. Has He said, and will He not do? Or has He spoken, and will He not make it good?"*
>
> *[Numbers 23:19]*

In this scripture, we can clearly see that God does not lie and there is certainly no need for Him to repent because He is a faultless God. God does not need to change because He is already without weakness and there is no darkness in Him. You would only need to change something if there is something wrong with it or if you are not happy with it. God is happy with Himself because He is immaculately unscathed and totally complete -

> *"For I am the LORD, I do not change; therefore you are not consumed, O sons of Jacob."*
>
> *[Malachi 3:6]*

As much as this scripture might seem a little contradictory, nevertheless, it will help us to understand that though God knew that the world would become sinful, He still chose to create us because He loved us even before He made us. That is why the latter part of the scripture says *"therefore, you are not consumed.''* This means that if God was to constantly change His mind like us, we would all be destroyed.

> *"All who dwell on the earth will worship him, whose names have not been written in the Book of Life of the Lamb slain from the foundation of the world."*
> *[Revelation 13:8]*

The scripture helps us to know that Christ the lamb was slain from the foundation of the world which means that God already knew that sin was going to enter into the world through the disobedience of man; therefore, God had already planned that He would send His only begotten Son to die and shed His blood for us in order to deliver us from the hands of sin. *[Isaiah 46:10/Hebrews 13:8]*

Artists often erase the unwanted parts of their work when it goes wrong or if it does not resemble the desired effect. Sometimes, artists completely tear the page out and create a brand new image on a different page, especially if they are not very pleased with what they see. When builders discover cracks and dampness in walls, they fill in all the cracks and eradicate every fault because it is a sign that there is a problem. This is a reflection of God's action towards mankind when He witnessed how they chose to be destructive as if He did not exist.

God decided to erase a significant part of the picture He drew and kept the little part that was good. The vast part of the picture was all those who did evil in the sight of the Lord and the small part that He saved, was Noah and his family whom He used as a seed to start again.

Can you understand God's point of view in this? Can you see how important it was for God to obliterate mankind from the face of the earth? You may ask yourself why didn't God use His power to stop the people from doing evil rather than choose to destroy them?

God did not change the people because He gave them free will; the ability to choose for themselves. This was why He gave them plenty of time to willingly turn from their wicked ways. God is still warning the world through His chosen prophets and through His Word so that those who heed His warning will be saved. However, it is up to the world to decide whose ways are perfectly true and whose ways are destructive.

Self Examination

Are you living a life that invites God's continuous warnings and judgement or are you living a life that qualifies you to be an object of God's favour?

Is your life a declaration of righteousness or a 'headache' to the Kingdom of Christ? Is your Christian lifestyle an inspiration to the world?

Let the above questions sink into your mind for a minute and see if there is anything in your life which is abominable to God and disqualifies you from stepping into the glory of the Lord. There may be certain pernicious things in your life that you might not yet be aware of, but it is important to conduct a personal investigation. If you discover anything, it is essential that you courageously demonstrate the necessary repentance by relinquishing every negative influence in your life. It is extremely important that we disentangle ourselves from activities which only cause us to fall into darkness. It is imperative that we do our very best to be as humble as possible and live the type of life which will be commended by God. *[1 Kings 11:1-11]*

The scripture tells the story of King Solomon who

was an honourable man in the sight of God until he got himself entangled with his many wives and concubines who turned his heart away from God, lured him into idol worship and so caused him to become a disappointment to God. The things we do and the people we converse with can persuade us to become 'children of disobedience'. It is extremely important that we apply godly wisdom to everything we do, so that we will not be bound by curses. We must not allow ourselves to be swallowed by the influences and activities of others in order to prevent us from doing the will of God. In addition, it is essential that we check ourselves thoroughly and ask God to help us to eradicate all the things in us that can easily pull us away from the presence of the Lord.

Perhaps you have some difficult habits that make you live a lifestyle that is similar to King Solomon's ways, but you are too caught up to pull yourself out; possibly as a result of peer pressure. In your case, it could be the occurrence of an ancestral curse that has been passed down and repeats itself in your life. Nevertheless, remember that you have the opportunity to break any generational bondage and set yourself free from sin by the power of the Holy

Spirit. *[Judges 6:25-2]* Therefore, do your very best to separate yourself from anything that would arouse God's anger and cause Him to implement judgment against you. *[Ezekiel 14:4-5]*

Admonition

It is important that we walk in humility in the sight of God all the days of our lives so that the glory of the Lord will always shine upon us. We do not have to wait until we arouse God's anger before we begin to humble ourselves because there are painful methods of chastisement that God can take us through in order to put as back on the straight path. God always wants us to be perfect like Jesus Christ who was without sin. Therefore, when God prunes us, He cuts away all the unnecessary baggage that is contributing to our failures and downfalls *[James 4:10]*.

We do not often understand God's methods or reasons, but His ways are perfect and true. When God purges us, He drains out all the filthiness from us and makes room for all the qualities that we need to live in His image. In the sixteenth chapter of the book of Numbers, we can see that the Israelites often needed to be disciplined by the Lord. Among the children of Israel was a man named Korah who experienced the wrath of God because he gathered many renowned men with him and they stood against the leadership of Moses whom God chose to be their Prophet. Their behaviour towards Moses was automatically against God's Divine order; therefore, God destroyed them. *[Numbers 16]* God's severe action against Korah and his followers was an act of pruning to eradicate the spirit of rebellion from among the children of Israel so that they would learn to be obedient *[Proverbs 13:24]*.

God wants to remove all the uncleanness, the painful past, the failures, and every disruptive spirit in our lives - in order to give us a bright and shining future. *[Psalm 31:23]* The standard of God's leadership does not make room for pettiness and sedition because God is perfect and He wants us to be like Him. This is why God uses some stringent methods to correct us so that we will eventually become whom He expects us to be. Growth is not easy - it takes time and experience because it involves many unique principles that we must earnestly practice until we mature into the people we were created to be. Korah and his followers would not grow under the leadership of Moses because of their pride and ambition. It is important that we always embrace God's laws and warnings because they will help us to be the best.

These wonderful principles are a tiny fraction of the mysteries of God that are revealed through His manifold wisdom. *[Proverbs 13:14]* God is always willing to help and restore anyone who takes the opportunity to come to Him. God is always ready to erase every evil from our lives and to recreate perfection in us, but only if we are willing to surrender ourselves to Him.

The End Of All Flesh

> *"Lamech lived one hundred and eighty-two years, and had a son. And he called his name Noah, saying, "This one will comfort us concerning our work and the toil of our hands, because of the ground which the LORD has cursed."*
>
> *[Genesis 5:28-29]*

Noah was born for a reason - just like the rest of us who are alive today as we all have our purpose in life. God has brought about our existence on earth to fit into specific roles that will change the world. History was made the day that Noah was born because God had a master plan which no one else could fulfil. God specifically designed Noah to be an instrument of deliverance - to save the world from doom. Likewise, history was made the day you were born. You are an instrument of hope and power. God specifically designed you for something that the world needs. You are here for a reason and it is especially important that you do the will of God and carry out your purpose in this world.

> *"And God said to Noah, "The end of all flesh has come before Me, for the earth is filled with violence through them; and behold, I will destroy them with the earth."*
>
> *[Genesis 6:13]*

When I read this passage, I wondered why God said those words to Noah, even though he was also 'flesh.' However, it occurred to me that at that point, God did not see Noah as "flesh" like the rest of the world because Noah was walking in the spirit which meant that he did not conduct himself according to the wickedness of mankind, but rather humbled himself in the sight of the Lord and stayed very close to God. *[Genesis 6:8-9]* This unique understanding helped me to acknowledge how God perceives us when we abide in Him. In addition, this means that if we obey God and surrender to Him daily, there will be no condemnation in our lives. *[Romans 8:1]* Noah's assignment on earth put an end to evil and made way for a number of people to experience the glory of the Lord. Conversely, God will use your assignment on earth to eradicate something that brings destruction and equally put in place something that has the potential to edify others and exalt the name of the Lord.

The Blood Of The Lamb

When the Israelites put lamb's blood on their door posts, the spirit of death passed over them. The lamb's blood was a sign of protection for the children of Israel because they were on the Lord's side. *[Exodus 12:6-12:13]* Therefore, your faithfulness to God will speak on your behalf and God will protect you from any disaster. *[James 4:10]* When you remain under the influence of the Holy Spirit, the judgment of God will pass over you. *[Romans 8:1-2]* It is important to educate yourself in the Word of God and continually pray that the awesome presence of the Lord will overshadow you daily. If you conduct yourself according to the principles of God, the Lord will keep you from evil and sanctify you as

He did with Noah and set him apart from the rest of the world. Remain faithful to God and He will show Himself strong in your life. Remain under the covering of the Almighty God and He will never allow anything to consume you. God is a very loving Father who always keeps His Word and never lacks anything. Walk with Him daily, rely on Him daily and remain in His shadow because without Him, you cannot conquer. Noah did not engage himself with the ungodly, thus he was highly favoured by God. Thus, when you walk in righteousness and holiness like Noah did in the sight of the Lord, you will be established in the blessings of the Lord. As the psalmist writes -

> *"Blessed is the man who walks not in the counsel of the ungodly, Nor stands in the path of sinners, Nor sits in the seat of the scornful; But his delight is in the law of the LORD, And in His law he meditates day and night."*
>
> *[Psalm 1:1-2]*

Chapter Two

The Ark

The Assignment

"Make yourself an ark of gopher wood; make rooms in the ark, and cover it inside and outside with pitch. And this is how you shall make it: The length of the ark shall be three hundred cubits, its width fifty cubits, and its height thirty cubits."
[Genesis 6:14-15]

Noah was over five hundred years old when God instructed him to build the ark. At that time, his sons were already of age, so he had some assistance to finish the project. Noah was old, but he still experienced the vibrancy of God because he found grace in the sight of the Lord. *[Genesis 5:32]*

"On the very same day Noah and Noah's sons, Shem, Ham, and Japheth, and Noah's wife and the three wives of his sons with them, entered the ark."
[Genesis 7:13]

Though, this scripture talks about the beginning of the flood---after the ark was built, it proves to us that Noah's sons were fully grown adults---enough to have their own wives. This also proves that Noah was already above the age of 500 years when God came down to tell him to put the ark together.

> *"You shall make a window for the ark, and you shall finish it to a cubit from above; and set the door of the ark in its side. You shall make it with lower, second, and third decks."*
>
> *[Genesis 6:16]*

According to the scripture, we can see that God specifically instructed Noah to build three floors in the ark. The three floors represent the levels of the Kingdom of God and its greatness. Moreover, it was because the ark was going to be a covering and a place of refuge for a multitude of people and creatures. The three floors in the ark are reflections of the first Heaven, the second Heaven and the third Heaven. *[2 Corinthians 12:1]* In addition, the Church has three levels – there are members of the congregation, there are Pastors/ministers, but the head of the Church is Jesus Christ our Lord who is the highest of all. Nevertheless, only eight people were able to enter the ark with the company of many animals. *[Genesis 7:13]*

Jesus Christ declared that -

"In My Father's house are many mansions; if it were not so, I would have told you. I go to prepare a place for you."

[John 14:2]

This is an indication that the Kingdom of God has plenty of accommodation for all of God's children. It was important for Noah's ark to have plenty of rooms - God wanted to save many people to come and dwell in the ark as well as the animals, but a major amount of humans beings did not make it into the ark because they refused to obey God. Conversely, those who refuse to do the will of God on Earth will not enter into Heaven.

But, what are the many rooms, you may ask?

The many rooms represent the many different offices in the Kingdom such as the Outreach Ministry, the Pastors, the Ushering Ministry, the Choir, the Catering Ministry, the Prayer Warriors or Intercessors.

It is extremely important for the Church to be the pinnacle and the focal point of everything in life because it represents God. God created the Church to reveal the Kingdom of God to the world and to reconcile all mankind back to God through the death and resurrection of Jesus Christ. Without the Church, the world would certainly perish. Without Christ and the influence of the Holy Spirit, no one would make it into the Kingdom of Heaven.

The Journey

> *"And of every living thing of all flesh you shall bring two of every sort into the ark, to keep them alive with you; they shall be male and female. Of the birds after their kind, of animals after their kind, and of every creeping thing of the earth after its kind, two of every kind will come to you to keep them alive.*
>
> *And you shall take for yourself of all food that is eaten, and you shall gather it to yourself; and it shall be food for you and for them." Thus Noah did; according to all that God commanded him, so he did."*
>
> *[Genesis 6:19-22]*

All the variety of animals from different territories of the world which God instructed Noah to gather was a symbol of all the lost souls in the world whom God saves and brings into His kingdom. In the same manner, the Church contains a colossal gathering of believers from different backgrounds, cultures and races across the whole world who come and fellowship together to worship the Lord. This is why the ark had to be very magnificently crafted.

The construction of the ark was one of the most extraordinary tasks in the history of mankind. Considering that technology was not so highly developed in those days, Noah's ark helps us to acknowledge God's phenomenal power and expertise.

Nowadays, mankind has developed the skill to build gigantic ships that involve a lot of technical engineering and mechanical ingenuity. Therefore, it is intriguing to ponder on the kind of method and the type of tools that Noah used to construct the phenomenal ark. What mode of transportation did he use to move around to gather the animals into the ark? Were the animals were within Noah's reach? All these questions lead us to acknowledge that God is awesome indeed.

During my research, I realised that many people presume that the ark was not as big as it says in the Bible and that it could not have maintained stability on the waters because of the lack of technology and expertise in those days. It would not have taken so many years of hard work and organisation if the size of the ark was just a fraction of what the Bible tells us.

The ark was so big that it would easily contain 36 lawn sized tennis courts on it and possibly three jumbo jets. The ark was certainly a huge vessel – enough to carry a hundred and twenty five thousand sheep.

Just cast your mind back for a minute and regard the amount of impediments which might have occurred in organizing the wonderful assignment according to plan. The amount of food supply that Noah gathered to sustain the animals was more than enough; it will also help us understand that God is mighty indeed because the ark was not an easy task to accomplish. Through it all, Noah still had to be responsible for his family. There must have been so many other things for Noah to do, but most of all, he was able to do what God instructed him to do because he totally relied on God's unfailing Power. Regardless of the experiences in his personal life, Noah accomplished God's mission miraculously.

Noah did not show any sign of anxiety because he knew that God was going to give him the power to complete the job - though he was aware that it was going to take some time and a lot of effort to build the ark. There is absolutely no way that Noah and his sons could have finished the great task in their human strength. It was the awesome power of the Lord that made all the difference. Indeed God is mighty and anything that involves Him is great.

Determination

Noah was a very old man when God called him to build the mighty ark to save many people from the flood. He was certainly old, but he patiently laboured with his sons to accomplish the great assignment. Noah could have used his old age as an excuse to complain to God, but because of his reverence for the Lord, he humbled himself and complied with God's instruction like a true servant. *[Genesis 6:22]* Surely, Noah must have known how great and difficult it was going to be to build the ark. The size of the mighty structure as well as the thought of an extraordinary gathering of wild beasts such as lions, tigers, elephants, birds of prey, amphibians, reptiles and stallions should have been enough for Noah to complain. In those days, the world was together as one enormous land and the oceans surrounded it.

This helps us to understand how Noah was able to move around without having to cross continents. *[Genesis 1:9]* Nevertheless, it does not mean that his escapades were effortless.

> *To Eber were born two sons: the name of one was Peleg, for in his days the earth was divided; and his brother's name was Joktan.*
>
> *[Genesis 10:25].*

The scripture tells us that the world was divided in the days of Peleg who was one of Noah's great grandsons. This was when all the nations were scattered all over the world and the continents were also formed, but in the days of Noah, it was not so. *[Genesis 11:1-10]*

One or two years of putting things together could have been more than enough for Noah to be justified in saying *'I have worked long and hard enough: I have waited long enough and I'm too old for this.'* He could have become frustrated with all the challenges to arrange everything according to God's specifications. Things could have gone wrong in some parts. A few things may have gone missing or misplaced. Not to mention that technology was not so elaborate in those days. However, Noah did not fail to complete his mission to the glory of God.

Firstly, let's focus our minds on the enormous number of trees that had to be cut down and be conditioned which must have involved a lot of time and effort. Again, it is imperative to take into consideration the long frustrating hours of hard graft and the many sleepless nights on duty. Imagine the aches and pains which must have been interminable indeed. Nevertheless, Noah did not compromise and he did not even try to revolt against God, but he acquiesced and remained navigable to his Maker. Eventually, the heroic ship was completed and it gracefully conveyed Noah's family and all God's creatures as it was constructed to do. It was not by Noah's own creativity, but by God's infallible wisdom and power. For any human being to have the strength, patience, wisdom, knowledge, tenacity and courage to perform such an immense duty certainly requires something that is far greater than the job itself. Noah could not have thought of building such a capacious vessel all by himself. It was certainly not by Noah's power that the tremendous ark was sustained and floated upon the waters until it settled on the mountains of Ararat *[Genesis 8:4]* This is a phenomenal illustration of the wonder of God; without the influence of His

Spirit in our lives we can never accomplish anything to His glory. It is by His unlimited and unfailing Power that miracles actually take place. Hallelujah!

Many would have chosen to boycott the great assignment and some would have given up half-way; others would have even ignored God completely because of the colossal amount of work involved. The thought of assembling a multitude of wild beasts from different places to dwell in the ark would have been enough for some people to resign. Noah paved the way for all of us who are alive today to learn how to completely rely on God's unfailing power. Noah's powerful legacy teaches us that if we totally accept God's guidance and allow Him to take us through the journeys in our lives, we will certainly triumph in everything we do.

Salvation: Jews And Gentiles

> *"Then he became very hungry and wanted to eat; but while they made ready, he fell into a trance and saw heaven opened and an object like a great sheet bound at the four corners, descending to him and let down to the earth. In it were all kinds of fourfooted animals of the earth, wild beasts, creeping things,*

and birds of the air.

[Acts 10:1-12]

In the life and ministry of the Apostle Peter, God used a very unique way to teach him about Salvation. Peter fell into a trance and had a vision about a vast collection of different types of animals on a large piece of fabric which came down from Heaven. God used the vision to let Peter know about his new creation that was going to be called 'Christians.' God used the vision to tell Peter to go and minister to the Gentiles that they might be saved and brought into the Kingdom of God. Again, this is an illustration of Noah's assignment to gather different animals to take refuge in the ark.

"And a voice came to him, "Rise, Peter; kill and eat."But Peter said, "Not so, Lord! For I have never eaten anything common or unclean." And a voice spoke to him again the second time, "What God has cleansed you must not call common." This was done three times. And the object was taken up into heaven again."

[Acts 10:13-16]

Peter was not comfortable with the idea of being among the Gentiles because it was against his Jewish culture. In addition, it was because the Jews perceived that all Gentiles were ungodly. However, God had to straighten out Peter's mind because He was going to use the Gentiles to establish the Church. This is often the problem with many Christians today, especially those who perceive themselves as perfect and holy - as if they already live in Heaven. This is how some Christians have convinced themselves that they are better than everyone else and have put themselves on a pedestal, as if all those in the world are filthy rags.

Truthfully speaking, there are many souls out there in the world who are more principled and Christ-like than some Christians who are already in the Body of Christ. In fact, some believers of Christ are only church-goers, seat warmers and miracle-chasers, whilst some are just following the tradition of their parents *[Hebrews 5:12]*. In other words, we have become so absorbed with titles and reputation so much that it appears as if we have forgotten what the Christian faith is all about. In this, many have put aside what Christ stands for and have become self-made judges and executioners - deciding who needs to be punished and who needs to be pardoned. This is often the case as some Christians have the impression that God is some type of punitive ruler who will destroy anyone who does not meet His requirements.

Therefore, a number of believers give themselves the right to place judgment upon others and condemn individuals, thinking that they are doing the will of God. This attitude is what has been preventing many congregations from growing individually and collectively as it is often presumed that all the souls who are not yet in the Kingdom are immoral. Many souls turn to the Church for answers, but many are failing to gain God's truth because we often accuse them of being wrongdoers such as whoremongers, thieves and fornicators when they come to us. It was not up to Noah to decide which animal should enter the ark. Likewise, it is not up to us to decide who is worthy to be saved. Anyone who comes to Christ is a new creation. *[2 Corinthians 5:17]* This is one of the many reasons why some souls are perishing.

As a matter of fact, some Christians in the Kingdom are experiencing failure because of the behaviour of other believers who appear to be more established in the Christian faith. For this reason some have been subjected to severe spiritual setbacks and made vulnerable to the devil. Such was the story of the man with the withered hand whom Jesus healed on the Sabbath day.

The Glaring Christian Error

"And He entered the synagogue again, and a man was there who had a withered hand. So they watched Him closely, whether He would heal him on the Sabbath, so that they might accuse Him. And He said to the man who had the withered hand 'Step forward'.

Then He said to them "Is it lawful on the Sabbath to do good or to do evil, to save life or to kill?" But they kept silent. "

[Mark 3:1-4]

The scripture tells us that the man with the withered hand was already in the place of worship when Jesus entered. This shows that the man with the withered hand was part of the group of people who were there to fellowship, but he was ignored because of his condition. As soon as Christ walked in, the congregation set their eyes on Him and they suspected that He would not turn a blind eye to the man with the withered hand. Jesus was angry in His heart towards them because their behaviour was contrary to what the Lord stood for. The Jews were not comfortable with the notion of healing the sick on the Sabbath day because it was against the law, there were other days on which they could have healed him and yet, the man was not healed. This proves that they had no excuse to criticise Jesus for healing the man.

> *"And when He had looked around at them with anger, being grieved by the hardness of their hearts, He said to the man 'Stretch out your hand'. And he stretched it out, and his hand was restored as whole as the other. Then the Pharisees went out and immediately plotted with the Herodians against Him, how they might destroy Him."*
>
> *[Mark 3:5-6].*

This is what happens in the in the Kingdom today, many souls are withering away and experiencing some severe circumstances, but they are often ignored as if they are insignificant. It has got to a point that a number of people are not accepted and honoured in their places of worship because of the lack of certain things in their lives. Many are in need of deliverance from spiritual oppression, but they are often demoralised and labelled as 'demonised' individuals. Some are in need of counselling as a result of the confusion they experience each day, but they are not taken seriously. Others are confused and distressed about many things in their lives that could potentially destroy them, but they do not have an answer to their problems because they are not perceived as important human beings. It is very ungodly to behave as if those that are sick and afflicted have nothing to do with the Kingdom. If we fail to show compassion to the feeble and refuse to do the will of God, the weak will continue to be withered and our journey in the Lord may come to nothing. I say this because Christ came to shed His blood to save us. It is extremely important that we do not use our liberty in Christ to disparage others.

Perhaps you have a friend whose prayer life is withering away, but you have often ignored him/her as if nothing were wrong. Perhaps you know a number of people who are financially withered, but they are often ignored and blamed for their circumstances. Maybe there is a situation in your personal life that is causing your relationship with God to be withered, but you do not know how to deal with it because you have been rejected by those who are supposed to counsel you and empower you to conquer.

> *"And behold, there was a woman who had a spirit of infirmity eighteen years, and was bent over and could in no way raise herself up. But when Jesus saw her, He called her to Him and said to her, "Woman, you are loosed from your infirmity." And He laid His hands on her, and immediately she was made straight, and glorified God."*
>
> *[Luke 13:11-13]*

Jesus came to emancipate the woman who was bound by the power and captivity of the devil. No prison can keep you bound when the Lord shows up for you. Nothing is strong enough to withstand the power of Christ. In Christ alone, there is justice, power, freedom and peace.

> *"But the ruler of the synagogue answered with indignation, because Jesus had healed on the Sabbath; and he said to the crowd, "There are six days on which men ought to work; therefore come and be healed on them, and not on the Sabbath day." The Lord then answered him and said, "Hypocrite! Does not each one of you on the Sabbath loose his ox or donkey from the stall, and lead it away to water it? So ought not this woman, being a daughter of*

Abraham, whom Satan has bound—think of it—for eighteen years, be loosed from this bond on the Sabbath?" And when He said these things, all His adversaries were put to shame; and all the multitude rejoiced for all the glorious things that were done by Him."

[Luke 13:14-17]

Jesus was disappointed because the woman was left alone in bondage for eighteen years. The ruler of the synagogue complained that healing should be done within the six days of the week, but not on the Sabbath day and yet, the woman was not delivered from her infirmity on any of those six days considering that she was bound for so many years. Perhaps you have been bound by the chains of severe circumstances, but you have been treated as if you do not exist. It could be that you are going through an indescribably difficult period in your life, but your situation has been used as a weapon to criticise and demoralise you. Sometimes it is difficult for Christians to acknowledge that the Lord does not show partiality because He loves all of us. In several ways, it looks like we have become gold medallists in being impudent towards each other, but non-achievers in practicing the will of God according to His Word. *[John 8:4-7]* The ministry of Jesus Christ is based on divine love, righteousness, holiness and power; it is certainly not based on human prejudice. It is not up to us to decide who deserves to be accepted and who is to be rejected, but it is very important that we embrace the Spirit of Christ and exhibit the fruits of the Spirit all the days of our lives. *[Galatians 5:22]* Too much focus has been put on outer appearances and status for too long. *[2 Corinthians 10:7]*

We have placed more emphasis on who is wealthy and who is not so much that it has left a very big gap in the Church. Therefore, people are not gaining the strength, the knowledge and the necessary spiritual tools they need to be effective Christians. It has become difficult for us to really grab hold of the principles that hold the Christian faith together because we have become lovers of hate and haters of love. Through this, many are falling back into sin because they have become strangers to hope and embracers of doubt. As a matter of fact, it appears as if we are failing to comprehend the marvellous mysteries of Christianity, as we have focused too much on reputation and status. This is what has been giving the devil the opportunity to build strongholds in the minds of many believers, especially those who are weak in the Spirit. We have the opportunity to gain full possession of the remarkable mysteries that the Lord our eternal Father has set before us. *[Ephesians 3: 9-10]* We have the power to make a mighty change in the Kingdom to the glory of the Lord.

Noah's ark was constructed physically and it would have been a place of worship for anyone who stepped into it. If all the unrighteous people had listened to Noah and joined him in the ark, it would have become their place of worship and refuge and they would have experienced the power of God. However, it was only Noah and his family who found refuge in the ark. Moreover, Jesus Christ also built his ark spiritually so that anyone who accepts Him as their personal Lord and Saviour will find refuge in it as part of His Kingdom. The Ark that Jesus built was and still is the Church, but it is not the buildings we worship and fellowship in, but the entire body of Christ across the whole world. The Kingdom is not for just a tiny group of people who are well-endowed financially or who occupy the best positions in the world, but it is open to everyone who is ready to accept the Lord and live according to the principles of God. *[Galatians 3:26-29]*

Therefore, do not judge who you think is moral and who is immoral because you are not perfect. It is not our right to decide who should come to church and should not. All human beings have something deplorable in them---no matter who they are.

> *"But God demonstrates His own love toward us, in that while we were still sinners, Christ died for us."*
> *[Romans 6:8]*

Christ came to shed His blood for us since the power of sin made us unrighteous and took us away from the glory of the Lord, not because we were perfect. Let us be reminded that we will only be made perfect when Jesus Christ our Lord comes back again. *[1 Corinthians 15:51-53]*

The Centurion

> *"There was a certain man in Caesarea called Cornelius, a centurion of what was called the Italian Regiment, a devout man and one who feared God with all his household, who gave alms generously to the people, and prayed to God always."*
> *[Acts 10:1-2]*

The story of Cornelius is a wonderful illustration to help us to gain some understanding that there are many individuals in the world who have the potential of God in them, but all they need is to accept Jesus Christ as their personal Lord and Saviour. Let the truth be told, there are many out there who have the love and the zeal for God and even carry the ability to proclaim the principles of God much more than some who are already saved. This is not to say that Cornelius did not believe in God because the scripture clearly tells us that He was devoted to God, but his story is relevant to many because He and his household were Gentiles who needed the Salvation of Christ. In this, we are made aware of Cornelius' noble character and his occupation as a centurion, which means that he was a commander in the Roman army. Being a commander in the Roman army is an indication that Cornelius was a man of valour, honour and discipline. Being a commander also tells us that he was experienced in battle and he had the expertise of weaponry and militant combat. A commander is fearless, focused, committed, ambitious, strong-minded and lawful.

"And from the days of John the Baptist until now the kingdom of heaven suffereth violence, and the violent take it by force."

[Matthew 11:12]

It is essential to have the ability to defend the faith at all cost; believers have the power and authority of Christ to stand firm against the wiles of the devil. The kingdom of darkness is working very hard to bring destruction to the kingdom of God; therefore, it is extremely crucial that we also become adamant in our faith in order to conquer the opposition.

> *"You therefore must endure hardship as a good soldier of Jesus Christ. No one engaged in warfare entangles himself with the affairs of this life, that he may please him who enlisted him as a soldier."*
>
> *[2 Timothy 2:3-4]*

As soldiers of Christ, it is imperative to live each day like spiritual warriors, but humble servants of the Lord. It is extremely important to be militant in the Spirit because we are in the middle of an unspeakable battle that cannot be fought with man-made weapons. *[2 Corinthians 10:3-5]* Cornelius' military expertise was a very credible asset to the Kingdom of God. In many ways, the lifestyle of Cornelius is a metaphor for how a Christian should be spiritually, as it is paramount for every believer to be a 'soldier of Christ.' Therefore, it is important to be militant and vigilant in our daily walks with the Lord so that we will not be weak and eventually fall. It is very likely that the centurion could have been the best armour bearer for the Apostle Peter.

Let God be glorified in the lives of those like our brother Cornelius whose history continues to impact many believers. We thank God that the centurion availed himself to be used to pave the way for those of us who today have the privilege to be Christians. God knows that there are many souls in the world today who are already fit for the Kingdom because they carry the qualities of Christ, but they are not known because they are not yet part of the Kingdom. Nevertheless, it is important that we obey the voice the Lord and reach out to the lost because many of them will be a great asset to the Kingdom.

"For all have sinned and fall short of the glory of God."

[Romans 3:23]

Every human being on earth daily falls short of the glory of the Lord in one way or another. There are mistakes that we make each day as the grace of God enables us to live. This is the reason that Christ had to come and die for all of us. If Christ had not shed His blood for us, no human being on earth would qualify to stay alive.

Let's not forget that even Pastors need the mercy of God daily and it is also important that they pray for themselves each day as well as they do for others.

"Then Peter opened his mouth and said 'In truth I perceive that God shows no partiality. But in every nation whoever fears Him and works righteousness is accepted by Him.'"

[Acts 10:34-35]

The Apostle Peter finally realised and understood the purpose of God and his prejudice toward the Gentiles was removed. Now, Peter began to look at the world from the point of view of Jesus Christ. From that time, Peter's mentality changed. It is extremely important that we learn to swallow our pride and humble ourselves in the presence of the Lord and passionately avail ourselves to do His will regardless of what we have known. The Apostle Peter obeyed the commandment of the Lord and journeyed to the house of Cornelius whom God had already visited. This tells us that we have no reason to doubt God when He instructs us to go in a specific direction to do His will. God will always go ahead of us and prepare things for us even before we reach where we are supposed to reach. This is why we have no reason to fear or worry about anything.

> *"The word which God sent to the children of Israel, preaching peace through Jesus Christ—He is Lord of all—that word you know, which was proclaimed throughout all Judea, and began from Galilee after the baptism which John preached: how God anointed Jesus of Nazareth with the Holy Spirit and with power, who went about doing good and healing all whom were oppressed by the devil, for God was with Him."*
>
> *[Acts 10:35-38]*

God's vision was fulfilled as Peter ministered to Cornelius and the people who were with him. This was the beginning of the Salvation of Christ to the Gentiles and this is what God meant when He gave Peter the vision about the different types of animals. Can you now see the assignment of Noah being repeated all over again in a different way through the Apostle Peter? Can you now understand God's heart towards the world?

> *"And we are witnesses of all things which He did both in the land of the Jews and in Jerusalem, whom they killed by hanging on a tree. Him God raised*

up on the third day, and showed Him openly, not to all the people, but to witnesses chosen before by God, even to us who ate and drank with Him after He arose from the dead. And He commanded us to preach to the people, and to testify that it is He who was ordained by God to be Judge of the living and the dead. To Him all the prophets witness that, through His name, whoever believes in Him will receive remission of sins."

[Acts 10:40-43]

The role of every Christian is to proclaim the Word of the Lord to the lost and give them the opportunity to experience the Kingdom of God for themselves. In this way, the whole world will also begin to do the will of God. At this point, I can see the impact of God's love in this world. God's endearing love has come very far from the days of our father Noah until now and it will continue to influence us until eternity. This tells us that God has not yet finished adoring us whom He created for His pleasure. As Christians, it is our duty to tell people about Jesus Christ our Lord who came to shed His blood for all of us. It is imperative that we impact the lives of all men and women across the world under the guidance of the Holy Spirit and let them know the good news of the

Lord our Saviour and great Redeemer.

The Perfect Footsteps

"The steps of a good man are ordered by the LORD, and He delights in his way. "

[Psalm 37:23]

As a Child of God, it is extremely important to follow the footsteps of Jesus Christ our Lord. Looking at the life of our Lord Jesus Christ, we can see that He travelled to many places; He did many wonderful things and attracted many followers who later became part of His Ministry in order to establish the Kingdom of God on Earth.

Likewise, everywhere you go and whoever you come in contact with, take the opportunity to let them know about the Kingdom of the Lord.

Jesus performed His first miracle by turning water into wine at a wedding in Cana in Galilee. *[John 2:1-11]* This means that if you avail yourself to proclaim the name of the Lord to people wherever you go, signs and wonders will follow you.

As long as you walk according to the guidance of the Holy Spirit, God can use you to cause a miracle to happen in someone's life. Perhaps you know someone whose lifestyle is equivalent to the situation at the wedding in Cana when they ran out of wine. It could be that you have a friend who no longer has joy in their life or perhaps you know a group of people who have lost hope in certain areas of their lives; it is the Word of God that can cause a miraculous change and restore joy into their lives. Nevertheless, do not perceive yourself as if you are Christ Himself because you are not. You are a child of God and a servant. Therefore, be humble and let God do His will through you.

The Bible tells us that when Jesus left Cana, He travelled to Capernaum with His mother and His Disciples. *[John 2:12]* From Capernaum, Jesus and His entourage journeyed to Jerusalem and He chastised the Jews who traded and gambled in the Temple. *[John 2:13]* There was a time that Jesus ministered to Nicodemus in Judea and from there He travelled to Samaria. *[John 3:1-21/John 4:3-24]* In all the places that the Lord set His foot on, He made people aware of the Kingdom of God. He impacted the lives of many who were willing to hear Him.

From Samaria, the Lord went to the pool of Bethesda in Jerusalem and He healed a multitude of sick people. *[John 5:1-14]* This is only a fraction of the many places that the Lord travelled to establish His ministry (His ark) on Earth. *[Acts 10:38]*

Jesus went to many places and He reached out to many people wherever He went. It is important to let your light shine wherever your feet may tread. You can make a difference at your place of work or any environment you frequent. Your presence can change individuals even if you are just standing at a bus stop. But, be careful that you do not do anything according to your own human strength. Sometimes, it is difficult for Christians to minister to the lost because they themselves can get burnt in the process by the fire of the devil, especially when they are not mature or strong enough in the Spirit. Therefore, it is extremely important to be under the guidance of the Holy Spirit because the fire of the Holy Ghost is much stronger than the fire of the devil. Once you are encamped in the fire of the Holy Spirit you can certainly withstand the devil's fire and anything else in the world.

In the New Testament, we can see that the Apostle Paul also went on many journeys and adventures across the Roman world to reach out to many souls and introduce them to the Kingdom of God. Paul experienced many harrowing situations on his travels, but he refused to resign from his duty in Christ. It is evident that the Apostle Paul's hard work in the ministry paved the way for many of us who are still alive today to testify of the glory of the Lord. From the book of Acts to Romans and Corinthians, we can find the great teachings of Apostle Paul.

From the book of Galatians, to Ephesians and Philippians, we can witness the history of the great Apostle. From the book of Colossians, Thessalonians, Timothy, Titus and Philemon, we can see the evidence of the magnificent impact of Paul's testimonies and powerful influence in the ministry of Jesus Christ our Lord. This was how the great Apostle followed in the footsteps of the Lord. However, this does not mean that you must deliberately force yourself to reach out to people because you will fail if you try to utilise your human strength; nevertheless it is good to proclaim the Word of God to as many people as possible wherever you find yourself.

All the works that Jesus did in the world before He ascended into Heaven symbolise His 'ark' because He continues to gather souls into His Kingdom through His chosen prophets. In addition, all the books that the Apostle Paul wrote in the Bible to teach us strongly continue to influence all Christians across the world. Upon receiving this knowledge, you have the opportunity to build your ark to the glory of the Lord. If you avail yourself, God can use you to be a wonderful inspiration to many individuals in the world today who are lost in their ways.

> *"And the things that you have heard from me among many witnesses, commit these to faithful men who will be able to teach others also."*
>
> *[2 Timothy 2:2]*

It is important to follow in the footsteps of Christ and the likes of the Apostle Paul and reach out to teach others about the principles of the Lord so that they will also come into the Kingdom of God and experience the goodness of our Maker and in turn, they will also become teachers and mentors of others. Therefore, do not be afraid, but avail yourself today and let the hand of the Lord be upon you so that all those who are lost will be found.

The Wise Master Builder

"According to the grace of God which was given to me, as a wise master builder I have laid the foundation, and another builds on it. But let each one take heed how he builds on it. For no other foundation can anyone lay than that which is laid, which is Jesus Christ."

[1 Corinthians 3:10-11}

It is evident that if you build something without proper planning, you could easily fall into despair. A house that is built inappropriately cannot be a proper home because it will not provide the suitable covering for its inhabitants.

"Now if anyone builds on this foundation with gold, silver, precious stones, wood, hay, straw, each one's work will become clear; for the Day will declare it, because it will be revealed by fire; and the fire will test each one's work, of what sort it is. If anyone's work which he has built on it endures, he will receive a reward. If anyone's work is burned, he will suffer loss; but he himself will be saved, yet so as through fire."

[1 Corinthians 3:12-15]

We have the assurance that we already have the skill

to be wise master builders because of the grace of God upon us. Jesus Christ is the only true foundation to build upon. If you build your ark upon Christ as the foundation, then the standard of your work is equivalent to gold. The whole world knows that gold is the highest and most precious metal because it is a very opulent item that is extremely dear to mankind. In fact, people have been known to go to extreme measures to obtain gold and others have even lost their lives because of its immense value.

One Step At A Time

"But if it is of God, you cannot overthrow it lest you even be found to fight against God."

[Acts 5:39]

It is important that you do not go ahead of God because anything you do which does not involve God's input will not stand. *[Isaiah 52:12]* If you rely on your own abilities, then you might become proud and become an offence to God.

No human being on earth can successfully do anything well without the power of God. Therefore, it is important to acknowledge that it is God who will give you the strength and divine direction that you will not experience failure along the way.

Remember that He will never fail you. Look back at Noah, he accomplished his mission successfully because he did not go ahead of God, but he complied with every instruction that the Lord gave him. Work according to God's procedure – do not be afraid to dream big and aim high, but be prepared to start small. Work hard, but wisely so that you don't kill yourself in the process. It is good to be zealous, but it is important to move one step at a time. Remember that Morning comes before the afternoon, the afternoon before night and night comes before dawn. Workers do not receive their pay before they work, but they get paid after they have worked.

You will not experience the aftermath of your discovery before its manifestation; therefore, work according to God's timing. *[Isaiah 52:12]* If you build too quickly and finish too early, then your work may come to nothing. If you take too long to start and take too long to finish, then your ark may have little significance.

Vigilance

> *"Then Peter took Him aside and began to rebuke Him, saying 'Far be it from You, Lord; this shall not happen to You!' But He turned and said to Peter*

'Get behind Me, Satan! You are an offense to Me, for you are not mindful of the things of God, but the things of men.'"

[Matthew 16:22-23]

It is imperative to be vigilant about your assignment in God because the devil will always try to prevent you from fulfilling your purpose. We can see that Jesus had to put His foot down and put Peter in his place because he became a stumbling block in His path. There are many cases such as this; there are many individuals in our lives who do not often see things the way we do and their opinions can deter us from moving in the right direction. In this case, Jesus stood firm because He realised that the devil was at work.

The devil can and will use people around you to discourage you from stepping into your destiny, especially if you are not very strong on your feet and not wise in the Spirit. This is why it is essential that you fully engulf yourself in the power of the Holy Spirit so that no plan of the devil will persuade you to sabotage your purpose in God. Also, remember that Jesus did not hold any grudges against Peter for being a stumbling block in His path to glory.

It is not necessary to be acrimonious towards people who make life difficult for you on your journey to triumph because it could slow you down. If you spend your energy becoming bitter against people, you may lose your focus. In fact, that is one of the many methods that the devil can use to entrap you. In other words, do not allow the venomous actions of others to persuade you to become a 'snake'. Snakes cannot stand high altitude because they are creatures of the ground. Therefore, if you become a snake, then God will not lift you up to where you are supposed to be because snakes cannot remain at the top.

I am sure you do not want to remain on the ground and eat the dust of the earth [metaphorically speaking]. But, if you continue to stay focused on what God has created you to do, He will surely lift you up like an Eagle and you will fly high above your enemies. When you become a defender and protector of your dreams and purpose in God, you will be a winner and a possessor of your destiny. Sometimes you'll be surrounded by persons whose cynical opinions may rub you the wrong way especially when they don't see what they expect to see. There are those who will often tell you things such as *''We will believe it when we see it''* or *''You are taking too long''* or *''Where is that thing that you said you would do, we don't see anything?''* or *''Take action and prove yourself.''* No matter how tempting things become, do not rush into your work and do not do anything to prove a point to anyone because it can destroy your assignment. Remember that Noah did not build his ark in the course of one day or one week and he certainly did not do it to please man, but He did it because God told him to.

"For it is God who works in you both to will and to do for His good pleasure."

[Philippians 2:13]

Acknowledge that the pressures that men will put on you to do something spectacular to please them will not bring you the kind of joy you are supposed to get from the accomplishment of your assignment in God. Therefore, be bold and trust God only because it is He who works through you to fulfil your purpose on Earth.

In addition, some will even continue to predict your failure and your downfall in order to pacify the passion in you, but do not allow any unfortunate suggestions to dissuade you from pressing toward your goal. Ironically, even your critics will benefit from the great blessings of your legacy.

Therefore, this is my personal advice to you - Be careful that you do not become like a speckle of dust in the wind, often scattered into the atmosphere like the feathers of a bird. Do not allow what bothers other people to be the same thing that bothers you. What makes other people who they are is not what makes you who you are. In order to do something to please people, you will have to become a different person. If you become a different person, you will not be able to accomplish your purpose. You can only complete your God-given assignment if you remain the person you already are because God designated your assignment specifically for you only to accomplish. It may appear as if you are making all the incorrect decisions in life, especially to those who do not understand or recognise your difference. Most people believe that they are important because of the possessions and the positions they have achieved, but many do not realise that they have succeeded in the wrong areas of life regardless of how endowed they have become. This is also an indication that they are not walking in the will of God to embark on their true purpose in life because they do not want to look as if they are failures.

There are powerful individuals who own several luxurious vehicles and opulent mansions, but they are not fulfilled. This does not mean that wealth is an ungodly lifestyle. However, you have the opportunity to make a big difference. Sometimes, the lack of certain things in your life may be seen as a result of your being irresponsible. However, doing the will of God is what makes you responsible. Likewise, it is the choices you make according to the Word of God that determines your maturity. Therefore, do not allow the negative influences of other individuals to persuade you to be someone else in order to do something else to look good in the eyes of people. Every human being is a hypocrite about something because nobody is perfect. Therefore, be the person who God says you should be, not whom people say you should be. It is important that you do not become a people-pleaser because you are here for God's pleasure. *[Galatians 1:10, Philippians, 2:13 Revelation 4:11]*

Persecutions will come from all directions; many afflictions, dishonour and provocations will come from numerous adversaries. *[2 Timothy 1:8]* You will experience many disappointments, aches and pains, but it is important to remain strong in the Lord and persevere. *[2 Timothy 2:3]* However, do not allow the spirit of bitterness to have its way in your life, but love, help, honour and edify others to build their dreams despite your own personal problems. Beware of different kinds of temptations that will come at you from different directions.

Do not allow the pressures of the world to overshadow your passion to build. It is very important to keep away from those who allow the devil to attack you, but stay very close to God and maintain a healthy relationship with people who genuinely love and respect you. Plus, surround yourself with individuals who are well experienced and equipped with the correct tools to assist you. *[2 Corinthians 6:14]* In addition, do not be ignorant of the devil's devices, but be fully aware of God's miraculous power. *[2 Corinthians 2:11]*

You may experience betrayal from some friends who are supporting you and who might become frustrated along the way especially when challenges appear to be impossible to deal with. *[2 Timothy 4:16]*

Do not be afraid of the mistakes you make; in fact,

being afraid to make mistakes is a fault in itself. Errors help you to identify what needs be fixed and what needs to left alone. In addition, they will help you to realise what needs to be replaced and what needs to be omitted from your life. Your mistakes can help you to know how efficient you are and how effective you need to be. Likewise they will help you to know what to learn and what to ignore. Moreover, having too many choices and decisions in your life can cause you to be confused within yourself. *[James 1:6-8]* It is important to count the costs, but at the same time, do not ponder too much about the expenditure because God is your provider and the supplier of all your needs. *[Philippians 4:19]* Nevertheless, encourage yourself in the Lord; acknowledge the power of your tongue and continually prophesy mighty things into your life by faith. *[Proverbs 18:20-21]* Finally, believe and trust that whatever it takes, God will empower you to succeed. *[Proverbs 3:5-6, Philippians 1:6, 1st Thessalonians 5:24]*

The Ark Of Moses

Jochebed crafted a small ark to carry and protect her newborn baby who was later named Moses. Moses' mother created the ark in such a way that nothing could penetrate it. Moreover, the small ark was strong enough to carry the little baby boy safely on the river.

"But when she could no longer hide him, she took an ark of bulrushes for him, daubed it with asphalt and pitch, put the child in it, and laid it in the reeds by the river's bank."

[Exodus 2:3]

We can clearly see in the Bible passage that Moses' mother used bulrushes which are very strong reeds. In addition, the scripture tells us that she daubed the ark with slime and pitch to make it watertight. Another way to describe "daubed" is "plastered" or "smudged;" also, slime is goo which is a sticky substance that acts like glue. Pitch is nowadays known as "tar" which is often used to build roads in order to withstand the pressures of the weight of vehicles. In the same manner, pitch was used to coat the outside and inside of the ark to protect it - to stop water from penetrating it.

In the book of Genesis, we can recall that Noah covered his ark both inside and outside with "tar" as a method of reinforcement. The great flood would have destroyed the ark if Noah failed to build it with the correct resources. Likewise, Jochebed's ark for baby Moses would have been consumed by the river if she did not craft it properly. Therefore, it is extremely vital that you build your ark effectively so that it will succeed in its great mission to the glory of the Lord. From Noah and Jochebed's experience, it is evident that no circumstance can consume your ark if you build it right.

"And his sister stood afar off, to know what would be done to him."

[Exodus 2:4]

The Bible verse above tells us that Moses's sister kept a close eye on the little ark as it floated on the river. This illustration is to tell you that God will keep a close eye on your ark regardless of the predicaments around it. Moreover, the baby in the ark was a symbol of all the generations who were going to come through Jochebed's lineage and all the multitudes of people whose lives were going to be impacted by Moses. This also, is a reflection of all the different species of animals which inhabited Noah's ark. This is why God wants you to build your ark – so that many generations will be saved.

"Then the daughter of Pharaoh came down to

bathe at the river. And her maidens walked along the riverside; and when she saw the ark among the reeds, she sent her maid to get it. And when she opened it, she saw the child, and behold, the baby wept. So she had compassion on him, and said 'This is one of the Hebrews' children.'"

[Exodus 2:5-6]

As Jochebed's ark caught Pharaoh's daughter's eyes, so your ark will attract the right people who cannot afford to turn a blind eye to it. Finally, when Pharaoh's daughter opened the ark and saw the baby, she had compassion on him. Likewise, when people catch a glimpse of what is buried in your ark, they will be touched and be drawn to it.

Discovering Your Ark

First of all, what will your ark be and how can you build it to the glory of the Lord?

Your ark symbolises your legacy, purpose on earth and calling in God. Your ark can be an invention you create which has the potential to change the lives of people all over the world. Your ark can be a book you write which will influence others to make Christ-like changes in their lives. Your ark can be a film you direct which inspires its viewers to become better people. Perhaps you have the ability to write powerful songs of freedom which can strengthen the weak and emancipate the oppressed. Perhaps you have an empty property that can be used for fellowship or as an actual place of worship, but you have allowed it to remain empty. Maybe you have a plot of land that can be turned into a farm which can produce food and generate business.

You can also use the land as a plot to build a school, a college, a hospital or a university by the grace of God. Ironically, the school, college, university or medical centre can also be your ark. Perhaps you have a vehicle that is big enough to carry a huge amount of people and it can be used for God's ministry.

Your ark could be an idea to set up a radio station to preach the gospel to a generation of people. It could be that you have the special skill to write poems of love which can help families and relationships to be healed.

In your case, your ark could be a unique investment that has the potential to break the back of poverty in your life and deliver your family and many generations from financial bondage. You may have the unique ability to turn angry and bitter people into calm and forgiving individuals. It can be your level of kindness, hospitality, compassion for others and your charitable deeds which can become a monument of inspiration to the whole world *[Acts 9:36/Acts 11:29]*

Maybe you are one of those unique individuals who has the ability to pray for hours; your prayer life can be your ark because your powerful intercession for others can make a very big difference and be a spiritual covering for others.

A very good example can be found in the great legacy of our father David whose strong history continues to stand firm in the Christian faith. David built his ark through his unique talents and his gifts which resulted in Psalms, Hymns and Songs of hope to the glory of the Lord. Another way that David built his ark was through his extreme submission to the Lord of Hosts. Today, the Psalms of David continue to strengthen our souls and have become a strong bridge that takes us closer to God. David's life experiences have become a perpetual ark of encouragement in my life because I am often very inspired to make a positive change and equally persuaded to do the will of God every time my mind recalls David's unforgettable history. What David built has become a strong pillar of hope and enthusiasm to a multitude of human beings across the world. *[1 Samuel 16-17]*

What you use your talents and gifts to create on this Earth can become great memorials of guidance to many who are in need of the necessary education in order to push them in the right direction. Therefore, learn to discover your strong points and allow the Holy Spirit to show you how to impact the world with what you have. *[1 Timothy 4:14]* It is extremely important to recognise the wonderful creativity of God in you and use it to build something that has the potential to motivate and transform generations. Without the correct foundations in your life, your ark will not withstand its test.

> *"Therefore whoever hears these sayings of Mine, and does them, I will liken him to a wise man who built his house on the rock: and the rain descended, the floods came, and the winds blew and beat on that house; and it did not fall, for it was founded on the rock." But everyone who hears these sayings of Mine, and does not do them, will be like a foolish man who built his house on the sand: and the rain*

descended, the floods came, and the winds blew and beat on that house; and it fell. And great was its fall."

[Matthew 7:24-27]

According to the scripture, it is important that you build your ark with the correct materials or the right tools so that it will not fail its test. It is imperative that you establish the foundations of your ark in Christ alone. It is through Jesus Christ our Lord that we have genuine strength; without the Lord nothing can stand. *[Colossians 1:14-17]* Christ is the Solid Rock; anything that exists without Him as the foundation can easily be torn down. *[Matthew 7:24-27]*

Nothing can overtake or consume you when great storms arise if you build your ark according to God's wisdom. Christ is our everlasting shelter who cannot be moved; He cannot be cracked or broken, but He can be leaned on for comfort, strength, peace, empowerment, healing, assurance and success. *[1 Peter 5:6-10]* In addition, Christ is our perfect protection and perpetual covering. Jesus Christ our loving Lord and Saviour is our eternal fortress who cannot be infiltrated. He cannot fall or be conquered because He is God. *[Psalm18:2]* Therefore, trust in Jesus Christ our Lord who saved us from the curses of darkness and let Him be the main substance which upholds your life and everything you build because He is the pillar and ground of truth. *[1 Timothy 3:15]*

Not By Might Nor By Power

> *"So he answered and said to me: 'This is the word of the LORD to Zerubbabel: 'Not by might nor by power, but by My Spirit,' Says the LORD of hosts.'"*
>
> *[Zechariah 4:6]*

You can begin this wonderful journey by rededicating your life to Christ especially if you have backslidden or are on the verge of it. *[Galatians 2:18-20]* In addition, surrender your life to the Holy Spirit so that the awesome power of God will become more effective in your life. *[Ephesians 3:16]*

When Ananias laid his hands on Saul [Paul], he was filled with the power of Holy Ghost so that he would be able to fulfil his calling in the Lord. *[Acts 9:17]* When we rely on the Holy Spirit, there is nothing that we cannot achieve in this world. When we abide in the Spirit and He abides in us, there is nothing that can defeat us. When the Spirit of God is with us there is nothing on Earth, above and beyond that can withstand us. As beloved children of God, it is indispensable that we humble ourselves and rely on the Holy Spirit. By so doing, the supernatural power of God will surely enable us to accomplish the greatest tasks and fulfil our destiny to the glory of the Lord. *[Deuteronomy 8:17-19]*

Secondly, feed your soul with the Word of God extensively because the Word contains all the correct substance to solidify your walk in Christ. *[Joshua 1:8]* Moreover, it is extremely important that you pay your tithes to the Lord and be gracious to the needy according to the Word of God. *[Malachi 3:10]* Learn to love your brethren; forgive those who sin against you and pray for other people as much as you pray for yourself. *[Matthew 6:14-15]* Be genuinely involved in the business of the Church and continually worship the Lord in Spirit and in truth. *[Acts 2:42-47 John 4:24]*

It is imperative to build your ark with the principles of Christ so that you will prevail. It is extremely important to be faithful and strong in the Lord through prayer and fasting so that you will remain standing in the midst of any flood, any storm and or stubborn situation that comes against you. *[Mark 9:29]*

May the Spirit of God guide you and help you to build your ark. May God give you the power to fulfil

His purpose on Earth. May your ark be established by God's truth. May the will of God be done in your life. Most importantly, learn to trust God all the way because He never fails. *[2 Corinthians 5:7/Acts 18:9-10/ Philippians 4:19]*

There is no accomplishment that takes place through human strength alone; there is always a greater influence that predetermines the breakthrough of our goals. *[Deuteronomy 8:17-19]* The knowledge and the power of an individual is never enough to reach an expected end; people have never been able to make it on their own without the correct help. It is evident that without the power of the Almighty God to keep us, we wouldn't be alive today. Without the awesome grace of God, no-one would have the ability to take a single step *[Proverbs 3:5-6]*

Without God's compassion, no human being could ever have the assurance to dwell in this world. It takes courage, strength and absolute faith to work for God because the assignments of God are great indeed. However, without the Spirit of God in our lives, none of us would have the endowment to execute or complete anything effectively *[Joshua 1:6-7/2 Timothy 1:7*] As long as we humble ourselves before

God and surrender to His unfailing Power, we will certainly triumph and walk in the glory of the Lord *[Proverbs 15:33 James 4:10]*

Chapter Three

The Flood

"And behold, I Myself am bringing floodwaters on the earth, to destroy from under heaven all flesh in which is the breath of life; everything that is on the earth shall die."

[Genesis 6:17]

The Definition

What is a flood and the reason for it? A flood is an overflow or an excessive amount of water or any liquid substance that has the potential to overwhelm whatever it comes in contact with. A flood can overwhelm mountains and mammoth objects that seem to be beyond measure. If there is an extreme amount of water in a lake, a river, a stream or if there is too much rain then you might get a flood.

Disaster movies and ecological documentaries give us a very good illustration of the colossal damage which floods can cause and the effects they leave behind. Considering the great Japanese earthquake and tsunami of 2011 the news footage we saw of that event was for many an eye-opening experience; the sheer destructive force was so evident, carrying great ships and buildings far inland. Floods have consumed major cities and villages to the point that many people have lost their lives, homes and businesses and became destitute. The most dreadful thing about a flood is that it cannot be easily stopped or contained by human efforts.

In some cases, great floods have been caused by melting snow which eventually became water and in turn, destroyed thousands of lives. There are floods that are also caused by landslides which eventually swallow up buildings and entire populations of human beings and animals. Landslides are not necessarily floods of water, but they are often made up of wet soil or 'mud,' but the aftermath is equally devastating. The damage which floods often leave behind can take years and cost billions of pounds/ dollars to rectify. A flood is a very fearful event because no human being has power over it; it is only God who is able to overpower it. Floods can toss the most gigantic ships and most commodious vessels to and fro like a little leaf in the wind and can totally level a huge forest into a flat land. A flood can very easily push the most immovable monuments and immense objects from one place to another. There is a force in every flood that no man can comprehend apart from God alone. God used the power of water to execute His judgment upon the Earth. Although, the flood was a very painful and terrible experience, it was a metaphor for spiritual cleansing. God saw that the world needed a thorough 'bath' because it was extremely plagued with abominations.

Spiritual Cleansing

Cleansing is a method that is often applied to eradicate dirt and obstinate odours in order to maintain neatness. God used the great flood to eliminate all the filth in the world because all the evil which man continually committed, produced a severe spiritual infestation which was an abomination to God. God was going to mop, wipe, scrape and rinse the Earth from all the filthiness that covered it.

> *"That He might present her to Himself a glorious church, not having spot or wrinkle or any such thing, but that she should be holy and without blemish."*
>
> *[Ephesians 5:27]*

Though this scripture talks more about the Church than the world, it focuses on the fact that God is a holy God and He has no room for filthiness. This also explains why it was important for God to wash the Earth from everything that was abominable in His sight. That is why the Bible tells us that *"God so loved the world that He gave His only begotten Son, that whoever believes in Him should not perish but have everlasting life."* [John 3:16] Despite all the callousness that occurred in the days of Noah, the world was very precious to God that is why Jesus Christ had to come because God wanted it to be clean and pure according to How He created it. This is telling us that God loved the world so much that He did not even want to create another Earth. God cherished it the way it was, but it had to experience some powerful cleansing in order for it to become brand new again.

Have you ever had something that was so precious to you that nothing else was good enough to replace it, even if the replacement was worth much more?

Think back to your childhood and recall a favourite toy or item of clothing and how nothing else mattered to you at all. Remember how precious it was in your own eyes, even more than your food, and you could not take your eyes off of it. Remember how that was the first thing you set your eyes on when you woke up and the last thing you looked at before you went to sleep. Plus, remember how you felt and how painful it was when someone else touched it the wrong way and made it dirty. This was exactly how God felt about the Earth and He did not want anything to tarnish it at all, but He rather created a solution to restore it to His glory.

The Benefits Of A Flood

A flood is not always a 'bad' event to happen no matter how disastrous it seems because it can shift good soil from one place to another. It can also persuade people to migrate from one place to another. A flood can turn a scorching desert into a fruitful land, as it has the potential to saturate the Earth. It is typically evident that when human beings are thirsty they quench their thirst by drinking water, fruit juice or other types of liquid from natural fruits such as grapes, pears and water melons. This is because the human body often experiences dryness like a desert and it is only liquid that can quench the dryness. Likewise, a flood has the potential to cure a land from drought, especially in cases of severe drought. Let us take a look at some examples to give us a better understanding.

"And Elijah the Tishbite, of the inhabitants of Gilead, said to Ahab 'As the Lord God of Israel lives, before whom I stand, there shall not be dew nor rain these years, except at my word.'"

[1 Kings 17:1]

By the word of the great Prophet Elijah, rain ceased to pour upon the land. We know that lack of rain causes drought which can severely affect a whole nation. In this case, water became scarce and a flood would have probably been appreciated because it would have at least created an opportunity for crops to grow. It was the rain that often brought fruitfulness to the Earth because it moistened the soil and made it easy to cultivate. However, when there is a great depletion of water, the land starves and the nutrients in the soil can die. When the land starves to death, it can make it impossible for crops to grow on it, especially if the crops do not absorb any water at all. Therefore Elijah's drought almost destroyed a whole generation. People were hungry for food, fathers, mothers and children were all devastated because the great famine threatened their lives.

The Power Of Abundance

"Then Elijah said to Ahab 'Go up, eat and drink; for there is the sound of abundance of rain." So Ahab went up to eat and drink. And Elijah went up to the top of Carmel; then he bowed down on the ground, and put his face between his knees, and said to his servant "Go up now, look toward the sea.'

So he went up and looked, and said 'There is nothing.' And seven times he said 'Go again'. Then it came to pass the seventh time, that he said 'There is a cloud, as small as a man's hand, rising out of the sea!' So he said 'Go up, say to Ahab, 'Prepare your chariot, and go down before the rain stops you.' Now it happened in the meantime that the sky became black with clouds and wind, and there was a heavy rain. So Ahab rode away and went to Jezreel."

[1 Kings 18:41-45]

The scripture above helps us to identify the importance and the necessity of a flood. Elijah knew that the rain which was going to fall was not going to be an ordinary rain because it was going to be a historical downpour, none like anyone had ever seen before. This was why he made Ahab aware that there was going to be an abundance of rain. Abundance means "a great quantity" or "an immeasurable amount of something." In other words, abundance is an amount that is difficult to calculate or measure. When there is an abundance of something, it means that there is more than enough to carry or more than enough to handle. When there is abundance, it means that even when everybody gets their share, there is still plenty to go around.

"But He said to them, "How many loaves do you have? Go and see, and when they found out they said, "Five, and two fish."

Then He commanded them to make them all sit down in groups on the green grass. So they sat down in ranks, in hundreds and in fifties. And when

He had taken the five loaves and the two fish, He looked up to heaven, blessed and broke the loaves, and gave them to His disciples to set before them; and the two fish He divided among them all.

So they all ate and were filled. And they took up twelve baskets full of fragments and of the fish. Now those who had eaten the loaves were about five thousand men."

[Mark 6:38-44]

This scripture is a wonderful illustration of abundance because the latter part tells us that the disciples still had twelve baskets full of food left even after Christ caused the five loves and two fishes to multiply into an immeasurable amount for the people to eat. This tells that the love that Jesus felt towards the thousands of people was in abundance; therefore, His response to their need was in abundance. This also illustrates the abundant love of God towards us; no man can measure the level of the love that the Lord feels for us. The people were empty with hunger, but Christ our great Redeemer cured their hunger with an abundance of food.

It is important to focus on God's mind in order to get a clear picture of why He caused the great flood to consume the Earth. It was all because God loved the world so much that He had to cleanse it. When God looked at the world, it was as if there was a famine because there was an extreme lack of righteousness, but God used an abundance of rain to flood the Earth to cure it from unrighteousness. Likewise, the abundance of rain in the times of Elijah eliminated the great famine and it brought fruitfulness again.

God still wants to cleanse the world with His Word

through us. Every time we go out there to minister His Word to the unsaved, we give them the opportunity to become clean and brand new through Salvation in Christ. *[Matthew 10:6-8 28:19-20]*

The Blood Of Christ

The death of Jesus Christ on the Cross of Calvary gave us all the opportunity to be cleansed and renewed with the perfect blood of our perfect Lord. This is why it is extremely important that we apply the blood of Christ upon our lives daily because it also empowers and sanctifies. The blood of Christ is the most magnificent spiritual detergent that exists because it cleanses and purifies of our sins. *[Revelation 1:5]*

As the great flood consumed all the rebellious inhabitants of the world, but only Noah and his family were saved; it was a reflection of how Christ was going to shed His blood upon the earth to redeem us from the powers of darkness and save those who will accept Him as their personal Lord and Saviour. *[Romans 10:9-11]*

> *"And He said, 'What have you done? The voice of your brother's blood cries out to Me from the*

ground.'"

[Genesis 4:10]

Form the experience of Abel's death by the evil of His brother Cain, we know that blood has a voice and it speaks on behalf of the innocent. Abel's blood called out to God from the grave for God to avenge him. This is how the blood of Jesus fights for us and commands the protection of the Lord on our behalf. The Bible also tells us that the life of the flesh is in the blood; this is why the blood carries power. *[Leviticus 17:11]* When the blood poured out from Christ's pierced side, it did not just ooze out slowly or gently, but it gushed out with power and it poured onto the earth.

"To Jesus the Mediator of the new covenant, and to the blood of sprinkling that speaks better things than that of Abel."

[Hebrews 14:24]

The blood of Christ represents the flood because it washes away all sin and anything that does not glorify God, but it protects the righteous. Likewise, the flood carried Noah who was righteous, but it washed away the wicked and ungodly from the face of the Earth. When the blood of Christ is proclaimed, it does not compromise and it does not fail to accomplish its mission because it is the perfect and mighty blood of Jesus Christ, our Supreme Lord and Saviour who died for our sins.

The Way Forward

God chose to use Noah and his family to rebuild His Kingdom on Earth because of their faithfulness to Him. Moreover, Christ came down from His place in Heaven to save us who are now Christians and those yet to come to know Him in order to build His Kingdom on earth. However, those who continually choose to love the ways of world and surrender themselves to the powers of darkness will be swallowed up by the judgment of God. *[Revelation 20:15/21:8/22:14]* Therefore, it is extremely important that believers take every opportunity to proclaim the Word of God to the perishing souls in the world so that they will learn to surrender to God and receive the mercy and grace of the Lord. *[Mark 1:15]*

It is imperative that Christians develop the desire and the passion to promote the Kingdom of God as much as possible that way many will escape the unspeakable experience of God's wrath. *[Romans 10:1-4]* Everybody you know deserves the right to be saved into the everlasting Kingdom of our Saviour Jesus Christ. *[Mark 1:17]* Sometimes Christians make it difficult for unbelievers to fully acknowledge the salvation of Christ, especially when believers complain about their circumstances and speak negatively about the Kingdom of God. *[Acts 3:19]* Many lost souls in the world are quite sceptical about the faith because they believe that Christians are not genuinely godly as they appear to be. Nevertheless, we do not have to allow the poisonous opinions of the world to deter us because every day is an opportunity to change so that by the grace of God we will be able to prove the world wrong. *[2 John 1:4, 3 John 1:4]*

We are privileged to have a Saviour who is immeasurably impeccable and unquestionably mighty. No other god is worthy to compare to our God; no other god can comprehend what it takes to do what our awesome God is able to do. *[Psalm 15:4-8]* In fact, all the other gods are impersonators because they have no original power of their own. *[Psalm 24:1-2]* It was not the devil who said *"'let there be light'; and there was light."* *[Genesis 1:3]* It was not another god who created the angels of Heaven. *[Psalm 33:6]* It was not the word of another god that framed the worlds and upholds the universe. *[Hebrews 1:3, Hebrews 1:10]* Life without understanding can produce some very damaging situations that even the sharpest minds on earth cannot comprehend. God is the only god whose ways are without fault. The Lord is absolutely flawless because there is no darkness in Him. Trust in the Lord Almighty and acknowledge that it is only through Him that you can achieve anything in life.

Chapter 4

The Rainbow

Symbol Of Peace

In the aftermath of the great flood, God created a rainbow and displayed it in the sky. Nowadays, a rainbow is often associated with children's activities and accessories because it is recognised as a symbol of peace and love. However, the world has failed to fully acknowledge what a rainbow really stands for. If we begin to see things from a spiritual point of view, we will understand that a rainbow is a very powerful thing, but it has been misinterpreted for too long. A rainbow is a magnificent symbol because it was part of a very influential history which mankind often takes for granted. God created the rainbow as a sign of peace to establish a covenant between Himself and His servant, Noah. The rainbow was God's signature of promise to reassure Noah that He would not bring the great flood to consume the earth again. *[Genesis 9:1-17]*

A rainbow is a representation of many things because it is made up of seven different colours, but it mainly represents the peace after a storm or the quietness after a great tribulation. In addition, it represents the presence and the beauty of God because it brings joy to everyone who experiences it. Every time a rainbow appears in the skys, it creates a tranquil atmosphere and it even pacifies the most stubborn characters on earth. Such is the power of the presence of God; it breaks down any spirit of pride, it cures any ignorance and it turns evil into good.

In my childhood days, I noticed that a rainbow usually appears after a rainfall and I tried to figure out why it happens that way. However, writing this book took my mind back to the times of Noah and the great flood; then it occurred to me that a rainbow is like a period of rest and freedom from oppression. When the rain falls, the rainbow follows afterward and amicably covers the sky. Therefore, as the rainbow appeared in the sky before Noah after the great flood, the peace of God shone upon Noah and his family after He demonstrated His wrath upon all the rebellious inhabitants. This tells us that the flood was a representation of God's anger and power, but the rainbow was a reflection of God's loving kindness.

God Of All Continents

The seven colours of the rainbow are a representation of the seven continents of the world; God gave Noah a glimpse of the future which took into account all the different cultures that God was going to gather from the seven corners of the globe through the salvation of Christ.

Have you ever noticed that every continent in the world is represented by specific colours? For example, the continent of Africa is often represented by very vibrant colours like red, yellow and green. Every country in the world is represented by specific colours and they have their meanings which are exhibited on their national flags. This also shows the impact of God's rainbow upon all the nations of the world.

> *"And He who sat there was like a jasper and a sardius stone in appearance; and there was a rainbow around the throne, in appearance like an emerald."*
>
> *[Revelation 4:3]*

The Significance Of Colour

We know that a rainbow contains many beautiful colours, but many of us do not actually know the biblical significance of the colours.

Red

Expresses the colour of blood and the atonement for sin. *[Leviticus 17: 11]* The blood of Christ was the propitiation for us when He was crucified on the Cross. Without the shed blood of the Lord our Great and eternal Redeemer, we would all be consumed.

> *"Not with the blood of goats and calves, but with His own blood He entered the Most Holy Place once for all, having obtained eternal redemption. For if the blood of bulls and goats and the ashes of a heifer, sprinkling the unclean, sanctifies for the purifying of the flesh, how much more shall the blood of Christ, who through the eternal Spirit offered Himself without spot to God, cleanse your conscience from dead works to serve the living God?"*
>
> *[Hebrews 9:12-14]*

Blue

Symbolises the Heavens and heavenly grace. This also represents the presence of God. We know that the sky is often blue and it hangs over us like the roof of a house. Likewise, the presence of God hangs upon us and covers us like a roof over a house. It is also a symbol of our security in the Lord because the presence of the Lord is our eternal refuge. *[Deuteronomy 33:27]*

> *"And they saw the God of Israel. And there was under His feet as it were a paved work of sapphire stone, and it was like the very heavens in its clarity."*
>
> *[Exodus 24:10]*

Purple

Represents royalty and majesty or Kingship. This colour was very precious in the olden days because it was often worn by Kings. In those days, the colour purple was extremely costly and a highly honourable colour to have on your shoulders.

> *"Now the weight of the gold earrings that he requested was one thousand seven hundred shekels of gold, besides the crescent ornaments, pendants, and purple robes which were on the kings of Midian, and besides the chains that were around their camels' necks."*
>
> *[Judges 8:26]*

> *"And they clothed Him with purple; and they twisted a crown of thorns, put it on His head, and*

began to salute Him, "Hail, King of the Jews!"
[Mark 15:17-18]

During the time of Jesus' Crucifixion, the soldiers put a purple robe on Him to confirm His Kingship and they declared Him as the King of the Jews. However, He was not just the King of the Jews, but the eternal King of the entire universe. Jesus Christ is the King of Kings and the Lord of Lords - the Majestic and the Supreme Shepherd who has no comparison. There is absolutely none like Him who died and shed His perfect blood for us.

Yellow

Is used to represent Gold which signifies Divinity and God's Glory. Gold is used to describe God's divinity because the divinity of the Lord is pure and cannot be tainted. *[1 John 1:5]* Gold is often used to make jewellery and many decorative crafts because of its immense beauty and value.

"And you know that He was manifested to take away our sins, and in Him there is no sin."
[John 3:5]

"This is the message which we have heard from Him and declare to you, that God is light and in Him is

no darkness at all."

[1 John 1:5]

The scripture clearly declares that *"in him there is no sin."* There are no impurities in God because He is infinitely honourable. There is nothing ordinary or common in God. There is nothing in God that can cause us to doubt Him because He is impeccably spotless and unchangeable. His mind, His heart and His ways are unquestionably infallible. There is no doubt in God, there is no fear in Him and there is certainly no negativity in Him because He is indubitably the epitome of righteousness and holiness.

"The name of the first is Pishon; it is the one which skirts the whole land of Havilah, where there is gold."

[Genesis 2:11]

This was the first time that gold was mentioned in the Bible. God knew that gold would be used to gain wealth and power in life; therefore, He created it for mankind to prosper. The whole world is aware that gold is a very valuable metal that has the potential to empower those who own it with wealth. In the days of old, it was extremely difficult to obtain gold because it took a lot of time and effort to dig underground in order to retrieve it. In addition, gold represents the purification process we go through in our trials as Christians. Gold is one of the only metals that does not lose its colour, weight, nature or any other property when heated with fire. Genuine faith is the same way. In scripture, gold is also used to describe the strength and the faith of a Christian.

> *"But He knows the way that I take; When He has tested me, I shall come forth as gold."*
>
> *[Job 23:10]*

After you have gone through trials and experiences to mature you, then you will become like gold which is a symbol to signify that you have entered into the glory of the Lord. When you become like gold, you become better, purer, stronger and more significant than before - that is when you will be more profitable.

Green

Represents new or healthy life which also speaks of good prosperity.

> *"Ephraim shall say, 'What have I to do anymore with idols?' I have heard and observed him. I am*

like a green cypress tree; Your fruit is found in Me."
[Hosea 14:8]

The scripture focuses on "the green Cypress tree" which indicates fruitfulness and good health. Therefore, the colour of green has a very significant meaning and it is a vital aspect of the life of a Christian.

"The LORD is my shepherd; I shall not want. He makes me to lie down in green pastures; He leads me beside the still waters."
[Psalm 23:2]

In the second verse of this scripture, we can see that David was referring to God as his Shepherd who makes him lie down in "green pastures." Green pastures are a symbol of a fruitfulness or abundance. When you have God as your Shepherd, He will cause you to live in the most opulent places where there is no lack. God will always make sure that your life is full of the best nutrition so that you will never be short of anything good in your life. This is how powerful the colour green is.

"The righteous shall flourish like a palm tree, He shall grow like a cedar in Lebanon. Those who are planted in the house of the LORD Shall flourish in

the courts of our God. They shall still bear fruit in old age; They shall be fresh and flourishing."

[Psalm 92:12-14]

Indigo

Represents covering or a form of protection. Covering can be interpreted in many different ways. It can be a covering of a loved one from harm, a covering of sin, a covering of shelter to keep something from the rain, the heat of the sun or the bellows of the wind.

For the earth will be filled with the knowledge of the glory of the LORD,As the waters cover the sea.

[Habakkuk 2:14]

Just as God uses the clouds in the sky to cover the earth, He also uses His presence to cover us from anything that can harm us. God also promises to cover our sins in order to prevent us from experiencing shame. *[Psalm 32:1]*

"And the waters prevailed exceedingly on the earth, and all the high hills under the whole heaven were covered. "

[Genesis 7:19]

When you look at the oceans on the Earth from a

bird's eye point of view or from space, its colour becomes indigo which is a dark blue or deep blue, especially where the waters run deep. Likewise, it is impossible for us to see the creatures in the sea from above, especially the ones who find refuge in the corals. Just as the waters cover all the creatures under the sea even though we cannot see them, God's presence covers us and protects us.

Orange

It symbolises fire and the Holy Spirit. As the Disciples of Jesus Christ waited in the upper room, fire appeared upon the head of each of them who were in the room - a sign of the arrival of the Holy Spirit.

> *"Then there appeared to them divided tongues, as of fire, and one sat upon each of them."*
>
> *[Acts 2:3]*

We know that fire has an orange colour and it is a high temperature; likewise the Holy Spirit comes like fire and nothing can withstand His heat. We also know that the sun has an orange-like colour and it produces an immeasurable amount of heat which no one can comprehend except God. This is another reason why the colour orange is used to represent fire because the sun is like a burning fire and it is orange. Likewise, the Holy Spirit purifies like fire. *[Zechariah 13:9]* Therefore, orange is a very powerful colour because it represents something that is far beyond human comprehension.

> *"Also from the appearance of His waist and upward I saw, as it were, the colour of amber with the appearance of fire all around within it; and from the appearance of His waist and downward I saw, as it were, the appearance of fire with brightness all around."*
>
> *[Ezekiel 1:27]*

Therefore, remember that a rainbow is a symbol of God's atonement for our sins and a representation of His Kingship. From this, we also know that it speaks of His divinity and His glory as well as new life and prosperity. In addition, we know that the rainbow is also a sign of God's Holy Spirit and purification. Likewise, we can now see that the rainbow also signifies God's covering, protection and Heavenly grace. In total, the rainbow is God's signature and presence upon the Earth which was also a covenant for Noah and his family. From now on, when you see a rainbow in the sky, remember that it is a very magnificent demonstration of God's presence.

I saw still another mighty angel coming down from heaven, clothed with a cloud. And a rainbow was on his head, his face was like the sun, and his feet like pillars of fire.

[Revelation 10:1]

The Coat Of Many Colours

In the Bible, there is a wonderful story about a man named Joseph who wore a special coat of multiple colours which was woven for him by Jacob, his father. Joseph's coat was another reflection of God's rainbow and a symbol of the presence the Lord upon him. *[Genesis 37:3]*

You may ask why Joseph's father didn't weave an ordinary coat that was made up of just one colour. The beautiful coat was a powerful statement to declare that the hand of the Lord was upon Joseph because he was chosen by God for a wonderful purpose. Conversely, the multi-coloured coat that Joseph wore was a symbol of God's favour upon his life. The favour of God is a catalyst for greatness.

This is a reflection of what Joseph carried on him as a chosen vessel of God. All the colours on Joseph's coat were depictions of the rainbow which appeared in the sky after the great flood. In addition, the rainbow which appeared before Noah was a symbol of God's presence and His favour. The presence of God carries an overflow of greatness that cannot be fathomed by anyone because it brings so many wonderful blessings which you cannot contain. Likewise, every time you see a rainbow in the sky, it is a reflection of God's awesome and illustrious presence upon the earth. When the favour of the Lord is upon you, it will empower you to become a fruitful individual. The favour of the Lord has the capacity to elevate you into a realm that no human being can comprehend. However, do not allow God's blessings upon your life persuade you to be conceited, but be more humble in the sight of the Lord the more accomplished you become.

Humility Is The Way To The Top ...

Pride Is The Way to The Bottom

It is extremely important that you do not allow your freedom in Christ and your promotion in life to be an obstacle to others as well as yourself. King Saul tried to use his position as the King of Israel to prevent David from rising up in the Kingdom; therefore, he fell into the hands of destruction. *[Isaiah 31:2]* King Saul became a vessel of dishonour when he chose to use his empowerment as a weapon to oppress many citizens of the nation which God put under his authority. *[Proverbs 16:19]* Saul should have mentored David and given him the spiritual nourishment to be established in the Kingdom. David could have been King Saul's perfect protégé, but that vision was turned upside down because of Saul's envy. *[Proverbs 16:12 /2nd Timothy 2:20-21]*

Sometimes, we are threatened by the potential of those who look up to us, especially when it seems that we will lose our popularity. However, let us not deceive ourselves because no one can remain at the top forever. Others have to carry the mantle after us, whether we like it or not, especially when we die. It is not a bad thing to train someone to follow in your footsteps; in fact it is a privilege for another individual to sustain what you started. It was a huge honour for the great Prophet Elisha to contribute to the remarkable legacy of his master Elijah who was one of the greatest prophets. In fact, failure to train another person to follow in your footsteps is a sign of failure. Many are afraid that their protégés or successors might be more accomplished and receive more accolades than themselves; therefore, they try to keep it all the power and the glory to themselves.

''It is He who, coming after me, is preferred before me, whose sandal strap I am not worthy to loose. These things were done in Bethabara beyond the Jordan, where John was baptizing. The next day John saw Jesus coming toward him, and said, "Behold! The Lamb of God who takes away the sin of the world! This is He of whom I said, 'After me comes a Man who is preferred before me, for He was before me.' I did not know Him; but that He should be revealed to Israel, therefore I came baptizing with water."

[John 1:27-31]

We can clearly see in the scripture that John the Baptist gave all the credit to Jesus even before He came to the river to be baptized. It was an honour for John to re-direct people's attention to another person whom he greatly admired and he wanted the whole world to also admire Him. It was a great privilege for John the Baptist to announce that Jesus was more worthy than him and was equally delighted about the arrival of the Messiah.

"For I say to you, among those born of women there

is not a greater prophet than John the Baptist; but he who is least in the kingdom of God is greater than he."

[Luke 7:28]

Here we can also see that Jesus Himself acknowledged John the Baptist and made people aware that John was the greatest Prophet of all. It is extremely important that you do not take all the honour upon yourself. Humble yourself and understand that it is not about you, but it is all about Christ. Another negative example can be found in the life of King Jehoram who used his Kingship to do evil in the sight of the Lord. Jehoram was given a very powerful position which many men would have been extremely privileged to have, but he took it for granted.

"Now in the fifth year of Joram the son of Ahab, king of Israel, Jehoshaphat having been king of Judah, Jehoram the son of Jehoshaphat began to reign as king of Judah. He was thirty-two years old when he became king, and he reigned eight years in Jerusalem. And he walked in the way of the kings of Israel, just as the house of Ahab had done, for the daughter of Ahab was his wife; and he

did evil in the sight of the LORD."

[2 Kings 8:16-18]

An additional example was king Ahaziah who followed in the evil footsteps of his fathers, King Jehoram and king Ahab. King Ahaziah lifted himself up and he became a severe 'headache' to the nation he ruled.

> *"Ahaziah was twenty-two years old when he became king, and he reigned one year in Jerusalem. His mother's name was Athaliah the granddaughter of Omri, king of Israel. And he walked in the way of the house of Ahab, and did evil in the sight of the LORD, like the house of Ahab, for he was the son-in-law of the house of Ahab."*
>
> *[2 Kings 8:26-27]*

The Perfect Role Model

Christ our Lord did not behave as if He was better than others, but humbled Himself as a servant even to the point of great humiliation and death on the Cross for our sake.

> *"Who, being in the form of God, did not consider it robbery to be equal with God, but made Himself of no reputation, taking the form of a bondservant,*

and coming in the likeness of men. And being found in appearance as a man, He humbled Himself and became obedient to the point of death, even the death of the cross. Therefore God also has highly exalted Him and given Him the name which is above every name."

[Philippians 2:6-9]

The humility of Christ is priceless indeed; He is the epitome of godliness and contentment. *[1 Timothy 6:6]* The best way to fully accomplish anything in life is to imitate The One who came to die for us. The wisdom and meekness of Christ is unmatchable and it should not be taken for granted since we are not worthy. Let your exaltation be an opportunity to give God all the glory He deserves and do not use it to oppress anyone.

If you think you have already arrived even when you are just at the tip of your beginning, then you may not even make it to the top because you must be more abased, especially when you are at the top. I say this because Christ was originally at the top of everything, but He did not exalt himself. He already knew that He was above all things, but He did not live according to that title. Christ made Himself of no reputation, especially to give us the opportunity to rise up high above from down below. The Lord became a servant that we would be Kings. He took pain so that we would have peace and joy. Remember your small beginnings, where you came from and how far you have come.

> *"For who has despised the day of small things? For these seven rejoice to see The plumb line in the hand of Zerubbabel. They are the eyes of the LORD, Which scan to and fro throughout the whole earth."*
>
> *[Zechariah 4:10]*

Always bear it in mind that it is by the grace of God that you have the opportunity to experience the freedom to prosper. Jesus Christ our Lord could have used the most opulent and most advanced chariot to travel around. He could have draped Himself in the most jaw dropping attire ever, with mighty angels around Him in order to prove a point, but He did not do so. Therefore, do not utilise your elevation by God to prove yourself to others. It is imperative that you help the weak to be strong, but teach the proud to be meek, and help the lost to find their way. *[1 Corinthians 8:12]* Be careful how you treat others with your greatness; be careful how you use the favour of the Lord upon your life because God is more than able to cast you down like a fool. *[Job 1:21]* Be careful of the seed you sow into people's lives; if what you sow is evil, then you will reap a harvest of evil. If the seed you sow is good, you will gather a harvest of good fruit. Therefore, use your legacy as an opportunity to reinforce those who are in need of support so that they will also gain some stature. *[Galatians 6:7]* We are nothing in the mighty eyes of God; it is by the awesome grace of our Lord that we become significant individuals to His glory. We are only dust and clay in the hands of the Great Potter *[Ephesians 2:8/Romans 12:3].*

> *"So David said to Michal 'It was before the LORD, who chose me instead of your father and all his house, to appoint me ruler over the people of the LORD, over Israel. Therefore I will play music before the LORD. And I will be even more undignified than this, and will be humble in my own sight. But as for the maidservants of whom you have spoken, by them I will be held in honour.'"*
>
> *[2 Samuel 6:21]*

In King David's case, we can clearly see that he grew stronger in the Lord each day and his reverence for God became more elaborate as David became more established. David did his best to maintain his admiration for God, and he was not at all ashamed of doing what was pleasing to the Lord. Continue to spread the love of God and proclaim the wonderful name of the Lord Jesus Christ who came to shed His blood for us. Be grateful to God for everything He does on your behalf and everyone He brings into your life to edify you. *[Proverbs 10:22]* Sometimes, a little strength can cause us to lift ourselves up and abuse our power, especially if we fail to count the costs and forget our small beginnings as if we automatically had the upper hand. As human beings, we can potentially become very egotistical when we catch a little glimpse of God's promotion that is before us even before we experience the blessing.

Be content with what you receive from God because it is more than you can imagine, no matter how it appears to you. *[1 Timothy 6:6-7]* It is extremely important that you do not go chasing fantasies because they are disguises of destruction. Sometimes, your lack of satisfaction can lead you into the mouth of envy and bitterness which can easily persuade you to destroy what belongs to other people, especially when you compare what you have with what others have. *[Philippians 4:11-12, Job 1:21]* Lack of contentment persuaded King David to commit adultery and murder which brought a curse into his family.

> *"Then it happened one evening that David arose from his bed and walked on the roof of the king's house. And from the roof he saw a woman bathing, and the woman was very beautiful to behold. So David sent and inquired about the woman. And someone said, "Is this not Bathsheba, the daughter of Eliam, the wife of Uriah the Hittite?" Then David sent messengers, and took her; and she came to him, and he lay with her, for she was cleansed from her impurity; and she returned to her house. "*
>
> *[2 Samuel 11:2-4]*

Remembering God

It is imperative that you serve the Kingdom of God with your gains and God will continue to increase your prosperity *[Galatians 6:9]* The more you receive from God, the more generous you must become because God can take it all away from you quicker than you can blink your eye lids. The more successful you become, the harder you must work for God; encourage others to be fruitful and exalt the Kingdom.

"For this child I prayed, and the LORD has granted me my petition which I asked of Him. Therefore I also have lent him to the LORD; as long as he lives he shall be lent to the LORD." So they worshiped the LORD there."

[1 Samuel 1:27-28]

This Bible passage shows that when God blessed Hannah with a baby boy, she rededicated the boy to God and in fact, she took him to the house of God and left him there. Hannah remembered God and used her baby to bless the Kingdom of God because she knew that God had the power to give her another baby if necessary. Hannah did not underestimate God and she acknowledged that God could have easily taken the life of her baby if He wanted to because He has the power to both create and destroy. Therefore, Hannah humbled herself even more before the Lord and took the opportunity to give God the glory He deserved for the miracle He did in her life. Hannah could have easily exalted herself especially toward those who once persecuted her when she was barren, but instead she used her energy to praise the living God who never fails *[1 Samuel 2:1-10]*.

It is unquestionably important that we learn from Hannah's history because it is a very logical platform for all of us to stand on to acknowledge how to behave toward God in everything we do in our lives *[1 Samuel 1: 21-28].* The greater we become, the more we should remember God; the more successful we become, the more beneficial we should be to the Kingdom of the Lord.

> *"Then Noah built an altar to the LORD, and took of every clean animal and of every clean bird, and offered burnt offerings on the altar. And the LORD smelled a soothing aroma. Then the LORD said in His heart, "I will never again curse the ground for man's sake, although the imagination of man's heart is evil from his youth; nor will I again destroy every living thing as I have done."*
>
> *[Genesis 8:20-21]*

We can clearly see that as soon as Noah came out of the ark, he remembered God first by building an altar for God and he worshipped Him with a burnt offering. In addition, the Bible says the offering that Noah gave to God was a sweet savour to the Lord. Moreover, God said in His heart that He would not curse the ground anymore or kill all living things again. This passage really helped me to gain more confidence in Christ because I have come to understand that my attitude towards God is what will persuade Him to break curses and preserve my life. Therefore, Noah's offering to God continues to be a very strong statement of protection for mankind, even until now. The curse that Adam's sin caused God to pronounce upon the earth was overturned by the obedience and faithfulness of Noah. Your attitude in Christ can persuade God to break generational curses and preserve the life of your children, great grandchildren and beyond so that they will experience the glory of the Lord. It is extremely important that you remember God with your blessings; put God first in everything you do and He will be merciful and gracious to you. *[Matthew 6:33]*

Your Personal Rainbow

In this case, a rainbow represents the manifestations of God's blessings in your life. Therefore, your personal rainbow could be anything that God will use to elevate you to the pinnacle of success and prosperity. In your situation, it could the end of barrenness which means that you will be blessed with children. It could also be the end of poverty and unemployment in your life. Your rainbow could be a new promotion at work or a major pay rise. Perhaps it could be a new home or a new vehicle and cancellation of debts. It could be a deliverance from satanic oppression or the breaking of curses upon your life. Your rainbow could be an encounter with a loved one and an opportunity for marriage. Perhaps it could be the first time you give your life to Jesus Christ, if you are not yet in the faith. Your personal rainbow could be the resurrection of your prayer life and emancipation from backsliding.

When your rainbow appears before you, do not forget to give God all the honour He undoubtedly deserves. When God removes your singleness and gives you a husband or a wife to marry, it is very important that you dedicate your spouse and your marriage to the Lord. Sow more seed into the Kingdom of God on behalf of the blessing the Lord gives you. When your rainbow appears before you and God blesses you with financial breakthrough, it is imperative that you bless the Kingdom of God with your wealth as a memorial to God. Most importantly, do not take credit for anything that the Lord does in your life no matter how far you reach, how high you rise and how endowed you become. King Herod refused to give glory to God when God used him to give a very unique speech to his people. The Lord would have established King Herod in the Kingdom of Christ if he chose to give all the credit to God; nevertheless, he failed to humble himself and it resulted in a very unpleasant death. *[Acts 12:21-23]*

God commanded Noah and his family to be fruitful and multiply all over the earth in order to transfer His prosperity from Heaven and establish it on earth. In addition, notice that God made a covenant with Noah only when the rainbow appeared which was after the flood. God will always show up and grant you the favour to prosper when you have gone through 'floods' of trials and tribulations. God will not allow any death-defying floods in your life to consume you; remember that He is your protector. God never lacks, He gives exceedingly and abundantly beyond what anyone can imagine or measure. *[Ephesians 3:20]* Indeed, the glory of the Lord contains riches unknown to man *[Ephesians 3:16, Philippians 4:19].*

Trials And Tribulations: The Path To Glory

Jesus Christ our Lord experienced great persecutions on earth and died a very painful death on the Cross before He resurrected and ascended into Heaven *[Hebrews 12:2-3].* Conversely, Joseph severely endured many years of tribulation before he lived his dream *[Genesis 41:39-57].* Abraham and Sarah spent many years of their marriage in barrenness before they received their blessing *[Genesis 21:2-7].*

There are experiences that we must all go through before we can inherit the blessings of the Lord. There are specific paths we must pass through before we can enter into the favour of the Lord. God's rainbow will always appear at the right time after we have experienced our floods. We will step into the place of fruitfulness and the fullness of joy after we have gone through the land of lack and emptiness *[Philippians 4:6-7, Philippians 4:19].*

In the books of Exodus, Leviticus, Numbers, Deuteronomy and Joshua, we see how the children of Israel were delivered from the land of Egypt, but they journeyed through the pernicious wilderness for many years before they came to the Promised Land. Moreover, the children of Israel gained the opportunity to experience the prosperity of the Lord when they stepped into the Promised Land *[Psalm 30:5].* The four centuries of slavery in Egypt and the forty years in the scorching desert represents their flood, but they finally saw their rainbow in the Promised Land. Just as God was with Noah and his family throughout the great flood and they settled peacefully *[Hebrews 11:7],* likewise God was with the children of Israel from their time in slavery throughout their time in the wilderness until they settled in the Promised Land.

Whatever storms, floods and hardships you are going through, remember that the God who is mighty in all things is with you and it won't be long before your rainbow will surely appear before you. The time for peace will come, the time for healing and deliverance is just around the corner and the time for joy is on its way, but stay strong in the Lord and it will soon be well with you by the grace of God *[2 Corinthians 4:17].*

Testimony

During the writing of this book, I was a newborn Christian learning how to walk spiritually. Nevertheless, my life was caught up in numerous storms and painful situations which came to overwhelm me like a great flood. Events such as unemployment and business failure brought poverty and emptiness into my life, not to mention, depression, sleepless nights and the experiences of betrayal which knocked me down to rock bottom. But God was faithful. Many false accusations were thrown at me from different directions, but I did my best to maintain my focus. God covered me and kept me in peace through it all.

It was as if the reproach in my life was never going to end, but I continued as if nothing was wrong. Circumstances almost took me to the grave, but God's miraculous power has kept me alive to testify of His glory *[Isaiah 54:17]*. Eventually, friends and loved ones no longer remained friends and loved ones, but God was with me. The amount of distress in my life almost drove me insane, especially because my confidence was torn to pieces by the constant lack of progress in my life. In fact, I became like a lost and lonely child in the wilderness in search of his mother, but my Lord held me together.

In the process of it all, I remembered the life of Paul and how God transformed him from Saul who was once a dangerous villain into a dignified and prolific Apostle of the Lord. He was once confident in his own eyes and persecuted Christians, but when he encountered the Lord, he became a blind and vulnerable individual until the Lord employed him again as His vessel *[Acts 9:1-15].* Therefore, it was important for Paul to learn to lean on Jesus Christ for the rest of his life

> *"And He said to me, 'My grace is sufficient for you, for My strength is made perfect in weakness.' Therefore most gladly I will rather boast in my infirmities, that the power of Christ may rest upon me."*
>
> *[2 Corinthians 12:9]*

Consequently, when you are down at your lowest point, God will magnify Himself in your life. When it seems that you have been dragged into the pit of total darkness, God will be your shining light and your guide to the right path *[Psalm 27:1/Psalm 119:105].*

The Apostle Paul could not have been used by God to do His will without the assurance of Jesus Christ because his own human confidence would have let him down along the way *[Galatians 2:20].* Through this, it occurred to me that God used all the harrowing situations in my life as a flood to wash away my human confidence so that I might inherit the assurance of Christ. As soon as I discovered God's wonderful plan, I held my peace and drew closer to Him. By the grace of God, I rose again in the name of the Lord to live again under His guidance; He has been merciful to me all the days of my life so far. I am privileged to live with the assurance of my Maker who knew me before He formed me in my mother's womb *[Jeremiah 1:5].*

Your human strength will let you down along the way because you will get tired, but if you trust in the Lord and rely on him, there is nothing you cannot achieve in this world. By His marvellous kindness, I live to see another day and I gladly lift up the name of Jesus Christ my Saviour and declare that He is forever faithful.

Do not despise your difficult times and your small beginnings; those are the times that God will help you to identify enemies who are like needles in your eyes or like hot metal spikes under your feet. These are the folks who will not hesitate to cut your throat when you are down on your knees. Nevertheless, that is also when God will enable you to discover the ones who are genuinely like cushions on your back and like water for your thirst. They are the ones who will love you and sincerely help you to succeed all the way to the top. The time for healing, deliverance and peace will come as long as you remain steadfast in the Lord, regardless of the predicaments that come against you *[2 Corinthians 4:17].*

Therefore, this book is my ark to you by the grace of God and I am fully convinced that it will inspire you as much it enlightened me. May this powerful book be a platform for you to stand on; I hope that it will help you to sail through your treacherous floods. I expect that this book will help you to draw closer to God and enable you to discover your purpose in Christ so that you may gather the necessary courage to build your legacy for many generations to come. Therefore, stand strong on your feet despite what comes against you and the magnificent Lord of hosts will surely deliver you from anything which tries to destroy you *[Isaiah 46:4, Psalm 124].*

Waiting On The Lord

The floods in your life may be harrowing indeed, but remember that the God of unimaginable power is more than able to dry up every flood and enrich every wilderness in your life to His glory. It may be that the flood in your life is barrenness or poverty; remain faithful to God like Noah and God will show up for you at the correct time. Perhaps the flood in your life is unemployment, spiritual apathy, a multitude of debts or a number of curses which weigh you down. Let your mind be on Christ who shed His blood for us and remember that every shame, every limitation and every curse was nailed to the Cross. It does not matter how many bad influences are biting off big chunks of your destiny and make it difficult for you to succeed. Remember that God is mighty and He has the absolute power to make oceans appear in the wilderness for your sake *[Isaiah 43:19]*.

> *"Thus says the LORD to His anointed, To Cyrus, whose right hand I have held—To subdue nations before him And loose the armor of kings, To open before him the double doors, So that the gates will not be shut: 'I will go before you And make the crooked places straight; I will break in pieces the gates of bronze And cut the bars of iron. I will give you the treasures of darkness And hidden riches of secret places, That you may know that I, the LORD, Who call you by your name, Am the God of Israel.'"*
>
> *[Isaiah 45:1-3]*

From today, God will break every yoke in your life. He will open the way for you and He will give you the opportunity to cross over to where you will experience joy and fruitfulness. God is more than able to command kings and those in authority to give up their wealth for you. Anyone and anything in your life that has risen above you and hindered you from moving forward will be cast out by the awesome power of the living God. Anything that has been oppressing you will obey God's voice and bow down to His command in Jesus' name. *[Isaiah 54:17]* Stay close to God and trust Him with your life because He has the power to expose the treasures which have been kept in secret for you.

Wherever your new job is, God will reveal it to you. Wherever your spouse is, God will reveal that person to you. Wherever your new home is, God will show it to you. Whatever is fighting against you, God will fight against it for your sake *[Psalm 18:46, Isaiah 54:15].*

The flood situations in our lives could be God's way of washing away every fear, every doubt, every curse and anything which could destroy us. Therefore, do not allow the floods in your life to persuade you to become bitter because God knows best and He knows how to turn bad times into delightful moments. In addition, God can use the floods in your life to prepare you for a harvest; this is because when water covers a very dry land, it wets the soil and the soil of the dry land becomes fertile. Fertility has the potential to produce growth. This means that God will use the floods in your life to create fruitfulness. Therefore, be patient, humble and strong in the Lord and He will not disappoint you *[Proverbs 3:5-6/Isaiah 40:29-31]*.

Faithfulness

> *"Shadrach, Meshach, and Abed-Nego answered and said to the king 'O Nebuchadnezzar, we have no need to answer you in this matter. If that is the case, our God whom we serve is able to deliver us from the burning fiery furnace, and He will deliver us from your hand, O king. But if not, let it be known to you, O king, that we do not serve your gods, nor will we worship the gold image which you have set up.'"*
>
> *[Daniel 3:16-18]*

The Bible passage above gives us a clear indication that it is extremely important to remain steadfast in the Lord no matter what predicaments surround you. The faithfulness of Shadrach, Meshach and Abed-Nego was what spoke for them when they came face to face with unspeakable danger. The fiery furnace that they were thrown into was a symbol of their flood which could have destroyed them, but they refused to allow it to deter them from staying strong in the Lord. In the same manner, be steadfast in Christ and remember that God will surely show up for you at the right time.

> *"'Look!' he answered 'I see four men loose, walking in the midst of the fire; and they are not hurt, and the form of the fourth is like the Son of God.'"*
>
> *[Daniel 3:25]*

The ark came to settle upon the mountains of Ararat by the flood. Likewise, God will use the floods in your life to lift you up high and all your enemies will witness the glory of the Lord in your life. *[Isaiah 41:10]*

> *"Then the waters would have overwhelmed us, The stream would have gone over our soul; Then the swollen waters Would have gone over our soul." Blessed be the LORD, Who has not given us as prey to their teeth. Our soul has escaped as a bird from the snare of the fowlers; The snare is broken, and we*

have escaped."

[Psalm 124: 4-7]

God has the expertise to keep you perfectly unscathed even when you are caught up in the most uncompromising situations because He has the answer to all things. Remember how God kept Noah in perfect peace in the ark whilst there was extreme devastation upon the earth; the same God who spoke one word from His mouth and life began is the same God who will protect you from the hands of terror and speak fruitfulness into your life at the right time *[Proverbs 3:5-6].* Keep your mind on Christ even when you get tired of waiting on God. Remember that God used the ark as a covering for Noah and his family during the great flood; in the same way, God will use your faithfulness in him to cover you and take you through every 'flood situation' in your life until the end. It is only when your floods have come and gone that you will experience your rainbow which is a powerful symbol of God's glory *[Proverbs 29:25].*

Chapter Five

Declaring The Awesomeness Of God

Reverencing The Lord

> *"God, who made the world and everything in it, since He is Lord of heaven and earth, does not dwell in temples made with hands. Nor is He worshiped with men's hands, as though He needed anything, since He gives to all life, breath, and all things."*
>
> *[Acts 17:24-25]*

What wisdom do we have to create something out of nothing? You would most definitely find that you do not know where to begin, but God knows where to begin, where to end, how to begin and how to end.

Even our great inventions are all concepts that have been imbedded in us by the awesome God Himself, whether they be giant locomotives that run on seemingly endless tracks across the world from nation to nation, or majestic ships and cruise liners that convey people and goods across the mighty oceans of the world or the satellites that hang in the uttermost parts of our atmosphere.

> *"And He has made from one blood every nation of men to dwell on all the face of the earth, and has determined their preappointed times and the boundaries of their dwellings, so that they should seek the Lord, in the hope that they might grope for Him and find Him, though He is not far from each one of us; for in Him we live and move and have our being, as also some of your own poets have said, 'For we are also His offspring.'"*
>
> *[Acts 17:26-29]*

Considering the earth is a planet that moves at a colossal speed on its orbit and yet it is still sustained by the force of gravity and other elements that are incomprehensible to man, these grand cogitations are but a mere fraction of God's wisdom. However, they are exhibits of His phenomenal power and infallibility.

> *"Therefore, since we are the offspring of God, we ought not to think that the Divine Nature is like gold or silver or stone, something shaped by art and man's devising. Truly, these times of ignorance God overlooked, but now commands all men everywhere*

to repent, because He has appointed a day on which He will judge the world in righteousness by the Man whom He has ordained. He has given assurance of this to all by raising Him from the dead."

[Acts 17:29-31]

"God fashioned us in the palm of His hands and there is no other god who is able to comprehend His excellent ways. Therefore, imagine our awesome God and how magnificent He is."

[Psalm 119:17]

There are nearly seven billion people alive today across the face of the world and still increasing, yet the world has plenty of space in it to accommodate every person and every creature, including the entire population of trees. Notably, the mighty oceans are more than enough for us to realise the abundant power and greatness of God. As you read this little information, gather your thoughts, picture it in your mind as clearly as possible and ask yourself the following questions.

- Am I able to comprehend this?
- Do I even know how to contain God's fullness in my mind?

- Can I fully measure God who knew me before the foundations of the earth?

Certain individuals have authority over great nations, but they still lack peace and understanding because they refuse to recognise that power only comes from the Almighty God above and not from mortals below. Many people trust in their own wisdom so much that they have convinced themselves and parts of the world that power does not come from above. Such people refuse to grasp the fact that God is alive; He is the living God who designed and built the entire universe. These are the kind of people who refuse to give all the credit to God; therefore, they have decided to lean on their own understanding and concluded that God does not exist. God is phenomenal indeed and He is the only one who is capable of creating life.

The world must accept the truth that apart from God alone, there is no-one who has the capability to fathom the knowledge it takes to create. All glory belongs to God who keeps a record of every grain of sand and every follicle. The Sovereign God is the only one who has the blueprints for everything that exists, both spiritual and physical, on earth, above and beyond. No human being is wise enough to fully comprehend the complete power it takes to be God. It is extremely important that we humble ourselves before God and acknowledge that it is He who deserves all the glory *[Deuteronomy 8:17-19].*

The All Knowing, All Powerful God

Through this book, we have the perfect opportunity take another look at the world and learn to acknowledge that God is real indeed. God is excellent in power; He is so much more than any human being can comprehend and there is nothing in the entire universe that is worthy enough to compare to Him or fully explain His existence. God is everywhere at anytime; He is with me as much He is with you. He is in every country, every city, every village and every town. God can be in every house, every living room, every bedroom, every kitchen, every bathroom, every toilet, every closet, every store room and every basement. God can sit next to you in your vehicle on your way to work and be with your children whilst they are at school. God can speak one word from His mouth to change everything in your life because He is God. One breath from God can wipe out everything and wipe out the earth like a deflating balloon in the air; therefore, it is wise to learn to fear God only *[Proverbs 29:25].*

Our God is the incomprehensible, incandescent and a perfectly dignified Shepherd who never slumbers nor sleeps and He never fails. Feel the air around you, look up into the sky, feel the touch of the skin on your hand and acknowledge that God is mighty. Take a look in the mirror, look at your face or into your own eyes for a few minutes and you will see that you are fearfully and wonderfully made because you are made in the image of God who is awesome and above all things *[Psalm 139:14].*

Whatever strengths we have, whatever advantages we have, we must always acknowledge that we are not the ones who have the power to supply our needs. It is God who supplies our strength, our daily bread, the air we breathe, the homes we dwell in and even the careers we have. It is imperative to understand that the God whom we serve has everything we need in the palm of His hands and without Him we can do nothing. The ability to sleep and the ability to eat are blessings of the Lord; the ability to stand and the ability to walk are powerful gifts which cannot be created by any human being or any other god. The ability to think, the strength to work and the reason to live are phenomenal blessings which no one has the power to produce except the Lord Himself *[Deuteronomy 8:17-19].*

> *"The earth was without form, and void; and darkness was on the face of the deep. And the Spirit of God was hovering over the face of the waters."*
>
> *[Genesis 1:2]*

Were we alive to be witnesses when the Earth was without form? Do we even have an idea of what it was like? Can we even begin to imagine how the earth became what it is now? The earth was once void, but the supernatural power of God is what miraculously caused life to spring forth [*Genesis 1:3*]. There is no one who has the answer to this because it is all beyond human understanding. Our minds do not have the capacity to comprehend what it takes to walk in the footsteps of God to do what He is so easily able to do. It was by the power of God that the Red Sea was parted in the Exodus, an act which no human being could ever replicate *[Exodus 14:21].* It is through the power of God that you and I are still alive today to testify of His glory.

The Taste Of Glory

It is imperative to acknowledge that what you are yet to receive will be so much more than what anyone has ever given you in your lifetime. What is yet to come is greater than what came yesterday and what you are about to set your eyes on is more beautiful than what you have ever witnessed before. What you are yet to know is far better than anything you have known before and what you are about to lay your hands on will be more rewarding than anything you have ever touched in your lifetime. What you are yet to learn will be more excellent than what you have learned before because God is getting ready to take you higher and deeper into His fullness. What you are about to eat will be more delicious than what you are used to. Where your feet are about to tread will be more prosperous than anywhere you have ever stood or walked before and where you are about to lay your head will be more peaceful and more welcoming than where you have hitherto been laying your head.

The experiences you are yet to have will be more magnificent than what you have gone through before and the people you are about to encounter will be more helpful to you than anyone you have ever met before in your lifetime. As long as the grace of God is upon you, you will be more alive tomorrow than you have ever been before and what you are about to stand on will be much stronger than what you stood on yesterday. History will no longer repeat itself in your life so give glory to God for bringing you this far. What you are about to hear is more constructive than what you have heard before and what is about to be spoken of you will be more honourable than what has been said about you in the past. The endeavours you are yet to undertake will be more miraculous than any journey you have experienced before. God is as real as the skin on your body and the hair on your head. In addition, God is larger than the skies and mightier than the oceans.

If you can be anything, be the person that the Lord will always be pleased to walk with. Be the person whom the world will miss when you are gone.

Perhaps your floods have not yet come, maybe you are right in the middle of it all or perhaps yours has already come and gone. No matter how long and arduous the trials and temptations in your life appear to be, do not allow anything to stop you from being the person that the Lord will delight in.

Remember that as long as the Lord is on the Throne, your life will no longer experience lack or limitation. Therefore, let the grace of God enable you to be the individual whom the world has never seen before. It is a great privilege to be the person whom God can rely on regardless of your weaknesses, failures and circumstances. Do not be afraid to be the person with whom people can find love and comfort; however, do not allow the spirit of compromise to have its way in your life because it can cause a lot of destruction. It is extremely important to be the person whom Christ can use to execute justice and establish God's truth on earth. If you can be anybody, do not be afraid to be the person whom God can use to do His perfect will and exhibit the mysteries of God. Hallelujah!

The Lord is still performing wonders and He will never stop loving you because He is God. God is undoubtedly stronger than the unbeatable winds, brighter than the sun and more phenomenal than all the galaxies in the universe. Therefore believe in Him, stand strong on your feet and in faith; stay strong in the Lord and continue to be hopeful under the awesome grace of God *[Psalms 23:4]*. When you sit to eat and drink with friends or family, do it with joy and in confidence, with acknowledgement and understanding that God has blessed you indeed. When you sit with friends, colleagues or family members to discuss matters, let it all be about Christ and all the wonderful things He has done [*Isaiah 30:23*]. From today, anything you do in your lifetime should be a testimony and a memorial to God for His mercies, His marvellous kindness, His immeasurable love and everything He has done and continues to do and all the uncommon things He is yet to do in your life *[Isaiah 45:1-3/Psalm 85:1/Psalm 31:21].*

Glory be to God. Jesus is Lord!

www.ingramcontent.com/pod-product-compliance
Ingram Content Group UK Ltd.
Pitfield, Milton Keynes, MK11 3LW, UK
UKHW021052270726
13967UKWH00012B/630